HARCOURT Math

MW00355526

Teacher's Resource Book

Grade 5

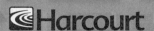

Orlando Austin Chicago New York Toronto London San Diego

Visit The Learning Site!
www.harcourtschool.com

ISBN 0-15-336867-5

3 4 5 6 7 8 9 10   073   10 09 08 07 06 05 04

CONTENTS

GEOMETRY

TEACHER'S EDITION PRACTICE GAMES

DAILY FACTS PRACTICE

FACT CARDS

VOCABULARY CARDS

IT'S IN THE BAG

Name _____

Problem Solving

Understand

1. Retell the problem in your own words. _____

_____

_____

_____

2. List the information given. _____

_____

3. Restate the question as a fill-in-the-blank sentence. _____

_____

Plan

4. List one or more problem-solving strategies that you can use. _____

_____

5. Predict what your answer will be. _____

_____

Solve

6. Show how you solved the problem. _____

_____

_____

_____

7. Write your answer in a complete sentence. _____

_____

Check

8. Tell how you know your answer is reasonable. _____

_____

9. Describe another way you could have solved the problem. _____

_____

Name _____

Problem Solving Think Along

Understand

1. What is the problem about?

2. What information is given in the problem?

3. What is the question?

Plan

4. What problem-solving strategies might I try to help me solve the problem?

5. About what do I think my answer will be?

Solve

6. How can I solve the problem?

7. How can I state my answer in a complete sentence?

Check

8. How do I know whether my answer is reasonable?

9. How else might I have solved this problem?

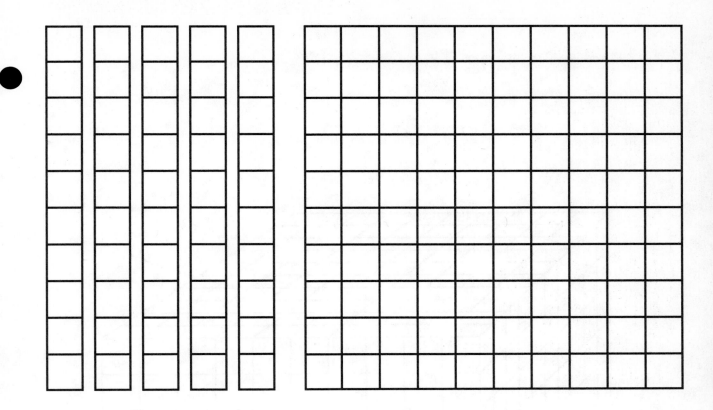

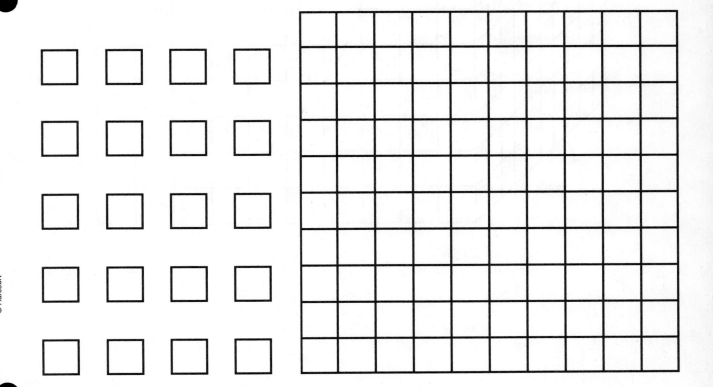

Base-Ten Materials

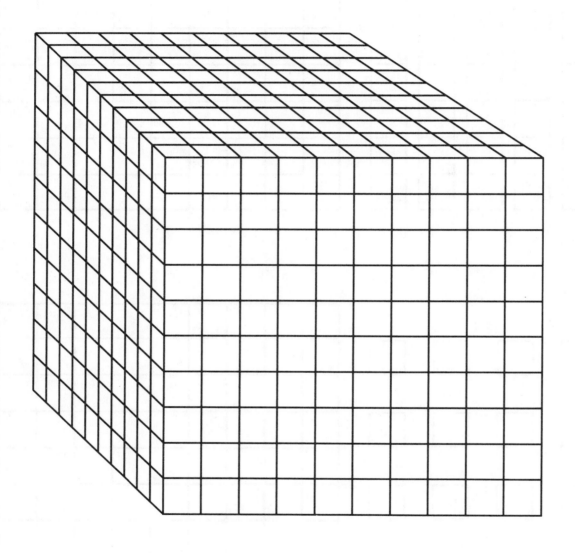

Base-Ten Materials

Place-Value Charts

© Harcourt

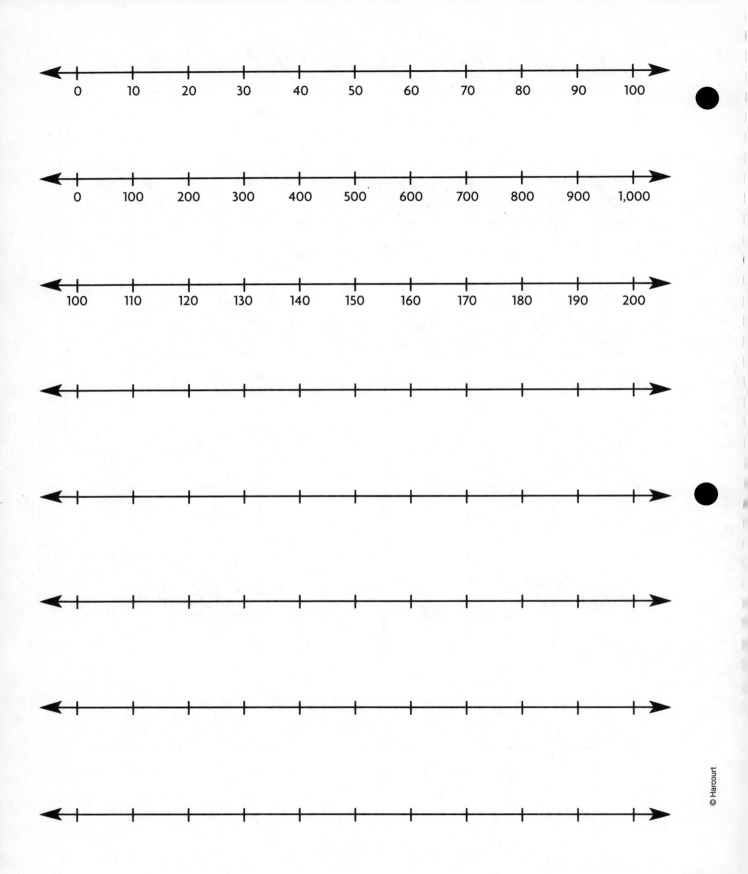

Number Lines

© Harcourt

	0	1	2	3	4	5	6	7	8	9	10	11	12
0													
1													
2													
3													
4													
5													
6													
7													
8													
9													
10													
11													
12													

Addition/Multiplication Table

×	1	2	3	4	5	6	7	8	9	10	11	12
1	1	2	3	4	5	6	7	8	9	10	11	12
2	2	4	6	8	10	12	14	16	18	20	22	24
3	3	6	9	12	15	18	21	24	27	30	33	36
4	4	8	12	16	20	24	28	32	36	40	44	48
5	5	10	15	20	25	30	35	40	45	50	55	60
6	6	12	18	24	30	36	42	48	54	60	66	72
7	7	14	21	28	35	42	49	56	63	70	77	84
8	8	16	24	32	40	48	56	64	72	80	88	96
9	9	18	27	36	45	54	63	72	81	90	99	108
10	10	20	30	40	50	60	70	80	90	100	110	120
11	11	22	33	44	55	66	77	88	99	110	121	132
12	12	24	36	48	60	72	84	96	108	120	132	144

Decimal Models

Decimal Models

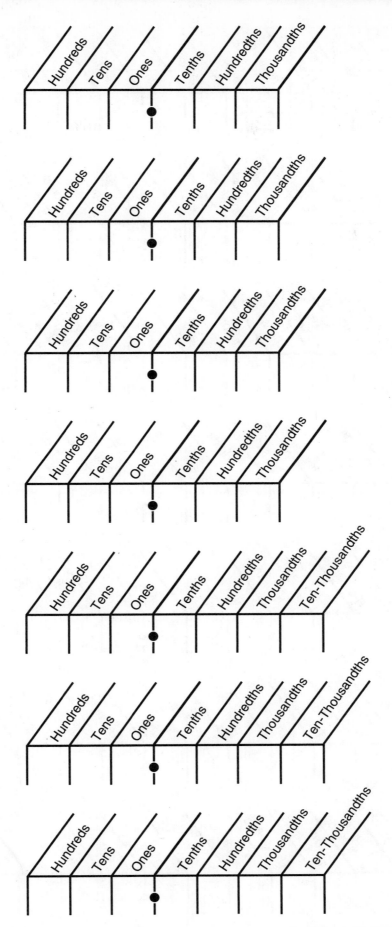

Place-Value Charts

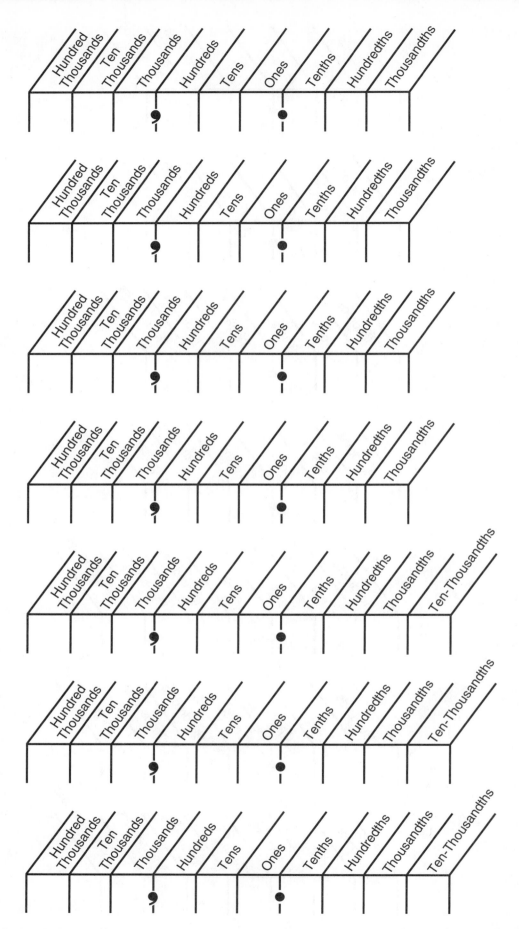

Place-Value Charts

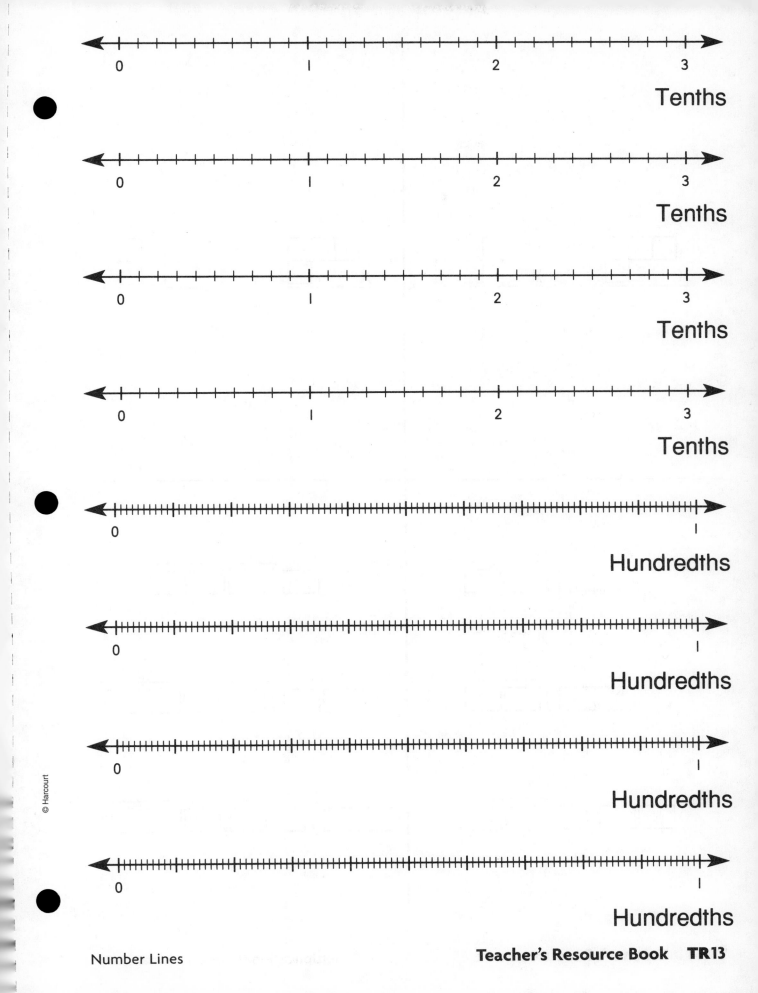

Tenths

Tenths

Tenths

Tenths

Hundredths

Hundredths

Hundredths

Hundredths

© Harcourt

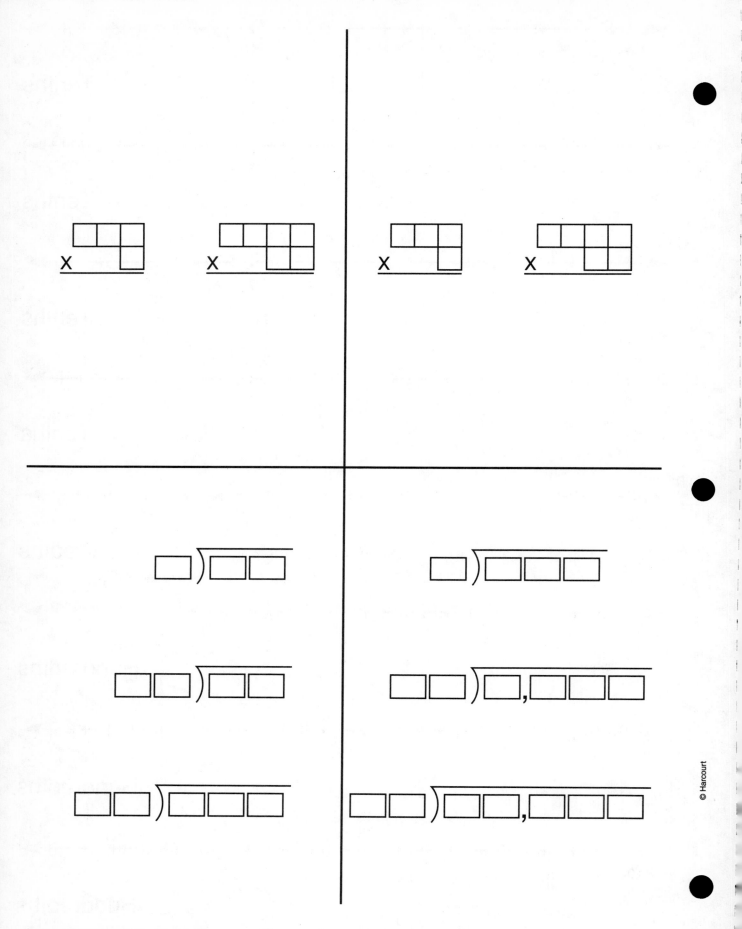

Multiplication/Division Format Boxes

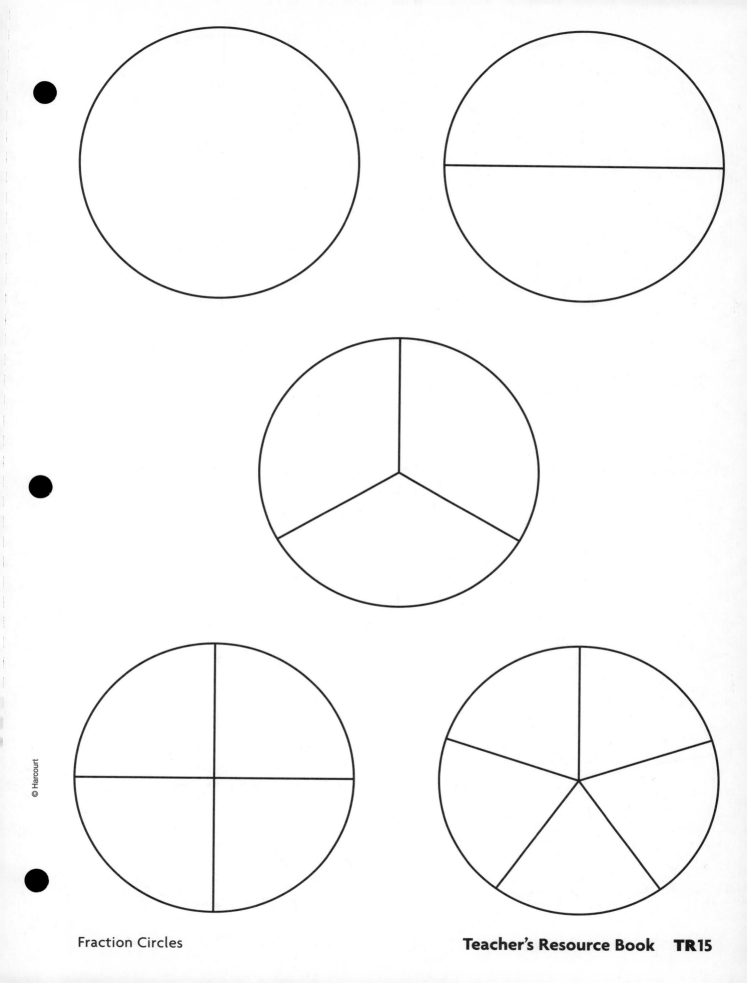

Fraction Circles

Teacher's Resource Book   **TR15**

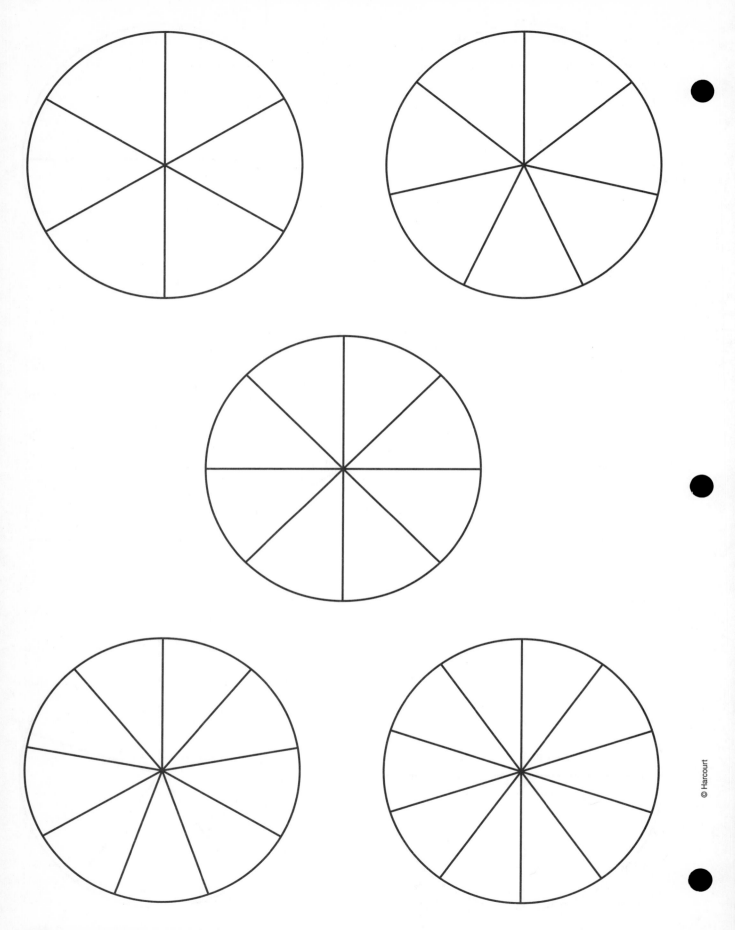

Fraction Circles

© Harcourt

| $\frac{1}{12}$ | $\frac{1}{12}$ | $\frac{1}{12}$ | $\frac{1}{12}$ | $\frac{1}{12}$ | $\frac{1}{12}$ | $\frac{1}{12}$ | $\frac{1}{12}$ | $\frac{1}{12}$ | $\frac{1}{12}$ | $\frac{1}{12}$ | $\frac{1}{12}$ |

| $\frac{1}{11}$ | $\frac{1}{11}$ | $\frac{1}{11}$ | $\frac{1}{11}$ | $\frac{1}{11}$ | $\frac{1}{11}$ | $\frac{1}{11}$ | $\frac{1}{11}$ | $\frac{1}{11}$ | $\frac{1}{11}$ | $\frac{1}{11}$ |

| $\frac{1}{10}$ | $\frac{1}{10}$ | $\frac{1}{10}$ | $\frac{1}{10}$ | $\frac{1}{10}$ | $\frac{1}{10}$ | $\frac{1}{10}$ | $\frac{1}{10}$ | $\frac{1}{10}$ | $\frac{1}{10}$ |

| $\frac{1}{9}$ | $\frac{1}{9}$ | $\frac{1}{9}$ | $\frac{1}{9}$ | $\frac{1}{9}$ | $\frac{1}{9}$ | $\frac{1}{9}$ | $\frac{1}{9}$ | $\frac{1}{9}$ |

| $\frac{1}{8}$ | $\frac{1}{8}$ | $\frac{1}{8}$ | $\frac{1}{8}$ | $\frac{1}{8}$ | $\frac{1}{8}$ | $\frac{1}{8}$ | $\frac{1}{8}$ |

| $\frac{1}{7}$ | $\frac{1}{7}$ | $\frac{1}{7}$ | $\frac{1}{7}$ | $\frac{1}{7}$ | $\frac{1}{7}$ | $\frac{1}{7}$ |

| $\frac{1}{6}$ | $\frac{1}{6}$ | $\frac{1}{6}$ | $\frac{1}{6}$ | $\frac{1}{6}$ | $\frac{1}{6}$ |

| $\frac{1}{5}$ | $\frac{1}{5}$ | $\frac{1}{5}$ | $\frac{1}{5}$ | $\frac{1}{5}$ |

| $\frac{1}{4}$ | $\frac{1}{4}$ | $\frac{1}{4}$ | $\frac{1}{4}$ |

| $\frac{1}{3}$ | $\frac{1}{3}$ | $\frac{1}{3}$ |

| $\frac{1}{2}$ | $\frac{1}{2}$ |

| 1 |

Number line 1: 0, $\frac{1}{2}$, 1

Number line 2: 0, $\frac{1}{3}$, $\frac{2}{3}$, 1

Number line 3: 0, $\frac{1}{4}$, $\frac{2}{4}$, $\frac{3}{4}$, 1

Number line 4: 0, $\frac{1}{5}$, $\frac{2}{5}$, $\frac{3}{5}$, $\frac{4}{5}$, 1

Number line 5: 0, $\frac{1}{6}$, $\frac{2}{6}$, $\frac{3}{6}$, $\frac{4}{6}$, $\frac{5}{6}$, 1

Number line 6: 0, $\frac{1}{8}$, $\frac{2}{8}$, $\frac{3}{8}$, $\frac{4}{8}$, $\frac{5}{8}$, $\frac{6}{8}$, $\frac{7}{8}$, 1

Number line 7: 0, $\frac{1}{9}$, $\frac{2}{9}$, $\frac{3}{9}$, $\frac{4}{9}$, $\frac{5}{9}$, $\frac{6}{9}$, $\frac{7}{9}$, $\frac{8}{9}$, 1

Number line 8: 0, $\frac{1}{10}$, $\frac{2}{10}$, $\frac{3}{10}$, $\frac{4}{10}$, $\frac{5}{10}$, $\frac{6}{10}$, $\frac{7}{10}$, $\frac{8}{10}$, $\frac{9}{10}$, 1

Number line 9: 0, $\frac{1}{12}$, $\frac{2}{12}$, $\frac{3}{12}$, $\frac{4}{12}$, $\frac{5}{12}$, $\frac{6}{12}$, $\frac{7}{12}$, $\frac{8}{12}$, $\frac{9}{12}$, $\frac{10}{12}$, $\frac{11}{12}$, 1

Number line 10: 0, $\frac{1}{16}$, $\frac{2}{16}$, $\frac{3}{16}$, $\frac{4}{16}$, $\frac{5}{16}$, $\frac{6}{16}$, $\frac{7}{16}$, $\frac{8}{16}$, $\frac{9}{16}$, $\frac{10}{16}$, $\frac{11}{16}$, $\frac{12}{16}$, $\frac{13}{16}$, $\frac{14}{16}$, $\frac{15}{16}$, 1

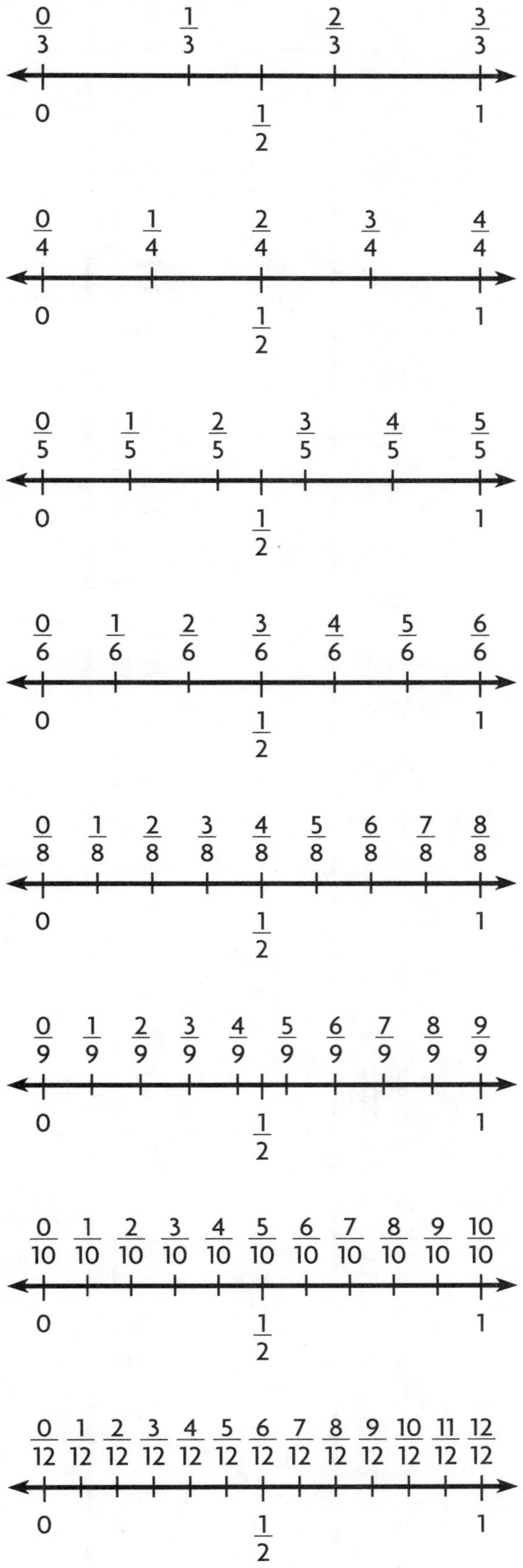

Number lines (left column):

$\frac{0}{3}$ $\frac{1}{3}$ $\frac{2}{3}$ $\frac{3}{3}$
0 $\frac{1}{2}$ 1

$\frac{0}{4}$ $\frac{1}{4}$ $\frac{2}{4}$ $\frac{3}{4}$ $\frac{4}{4}$
0 $\frac{1}{2}$ 1

$\frac{0}{5}$ $\frac{1}{5}$ $\frac{2}{5}$ $\frac{3}{5}$ $\frac{4}{5}$ $\frac{5}{5}$
0 $\frac{1}{2}$ 1

$\frac{0}{6}$ $\frac{1}{6}$ $\frac{2}{6}$ $\frac{3}{6}$ $\frac{4}{6}$ $\frac{5}{6}$ $\frac{6}{6}$
0 $\frac{1}{2}$ 1

$\frac{0}{8}$ $\frac{1}{8}$ $\frac{2}{8}$ $\frac{3}{8}$ $\frac{4}{8}$ $\frac{5}{8}$ $\frac{6}{8}$ $\frac{7}{8}$ $\frac{8}{8}$
0 $\frac{1}{2}$ 1

$\frac{0}{9}$ $\frac{1}{9}$ $\frac{2}{9}$ $\frac{3}{9}$ $\frac{4}{9}$ $\frac{5}{9}$ $\frac{6}{9}$ $\frac{7}{9}$ $\frac{8}{9}$ $\frac{9}{9}$
0 $\frac{1}{2}$ 1

$\frac{0}{10}$ $\frac{1}{10}$ $\frac{2}{10}$ $\frac{3}{10}$ $\frac{4}{10}$ $\frac{5}{10}$ $\frac{6}{10}$ $\frac{7}{10}$ $\frac{8}{10}$ $\frac{9}{10}$ $\frac{10}{10}$
0 $\frac{1}{2}$ 1

$\frac{0}{12}$ $\frac{1}{12}$ $\frac{2}{12}$ $\frac{3}{12}$ $\frac{4}{12}$ $\frac{5}{12}$ $\frac{6}{12}$ $\frac{7}{12}$ $\frac{8}{12}$ $\frac{9}{12}$ $\frac{10}{12}$ $\frac{11}{12}$ $\frac{12}{12}$
0 $\frac{1}{2}$ 1

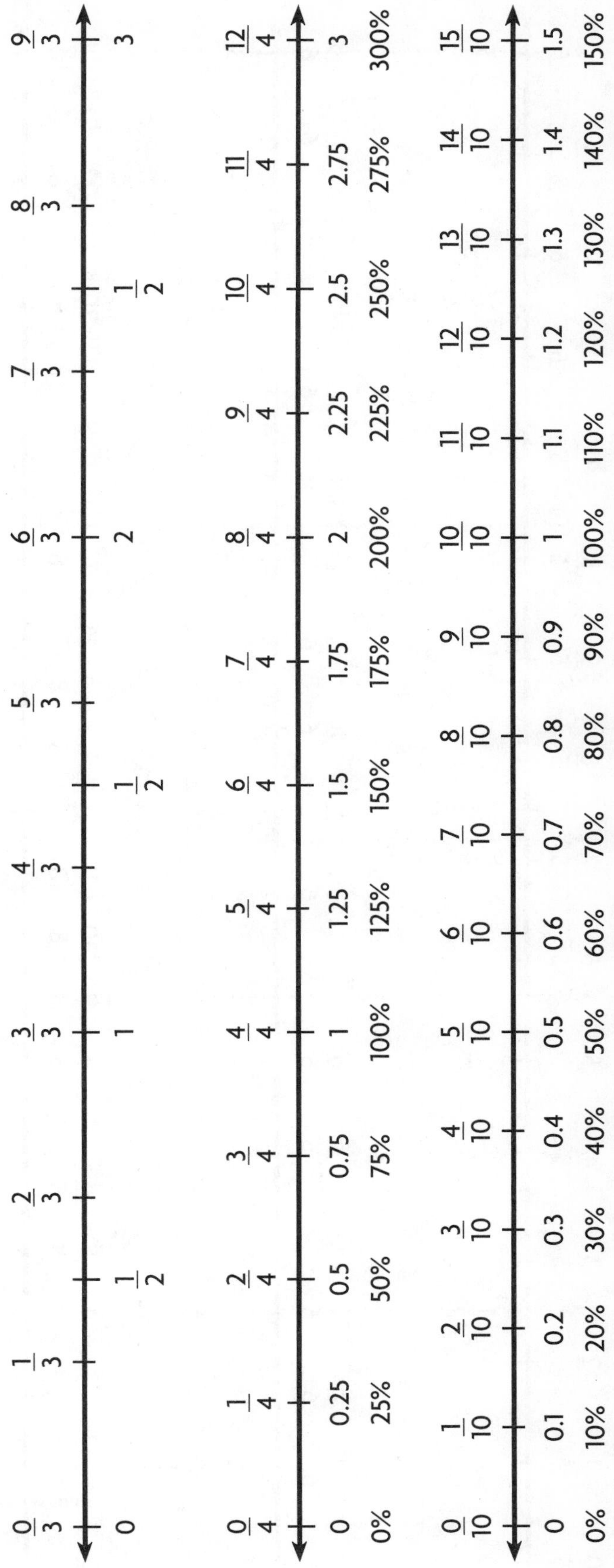

Vertical number line (thirds):

$\frac{9}{3}$ — 3
$\frac{8}{3}$
$\frac{7}{3}$ — $\frac{1}{2}$
$\frac{6}{3}$ — 2
$\frac{5}{3}$
$\frac{4}{3}$ — $\frac{1}{2}$
$\frac{3}{3}$ — 1
$\frac{2}{3}$
$\frac{1}{3}$ — $\frac{1}{2}$
$\frac{0}{3}$ — 0

Vertical number line (fourths):

$\frac{12}{4}$ — 3 — 300%
$\frac{11}{4}$ — 2.75 — 275%
$\frac{10}{4}$ — 2.5 — 250%
$\frac{9}{4}$ — 2.25 — 225%
$\frac{8}{4}$ — 2 — 200%
$\frac{7}{4}$ — 1.75 — 175%
$\frac{6}{4}$ — 1.5 — 150%
$\frac{5}{4}$ — 1.25 — 125%
$\frac{4}{4}$ — 1 — 100%
$\frac{3}{4}$ — 0.75 — 75%
$\frac{2}{4}$ — 0.5 — 50%
$\frac{1}{4}$ — 0.25 — 25%
$\frac{0}{4}$ — 0 — 0%

Vertical number line (tenths):

$\frac{15}{10}$ — 1.5 — 150%
$\frac{14}{10}$ — 1.4 — 140%
$\frac{13}{10}$ — 1.3 — 130%
$\frac{12}{10}$ — 1.2 — 120%
$\frac{11}{10}$ — 1.1 — 110%
$\frac{10}{10}$ — 1 — 100%
$\frac{9}{10}$ — 0.9 — 90%
$\frac{8}{10}$ — 0.8 — 80%
$\frac{7}{10}$ — 0.7 — 70%
$\frac{6}{10}$ — 0.6 — 60%
$\frac{5}{10}$ — 0.5 — 50%
$\frac{4}{10}$ — 0.4 — 40%
$\frac{3}{10}$ — 0.3 — 30%
$\frac{2}{10}$ — 0.2 — 20%
$\frac{1}{10}$ — 0.1 — 10%
$\frac{0}{10}$ — 0 — 0%

Number Lines

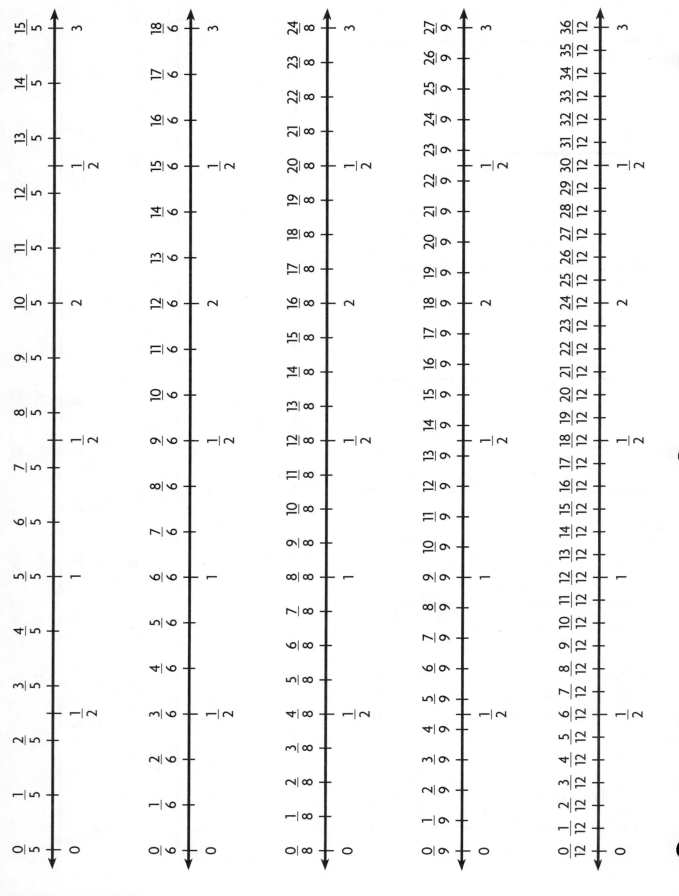

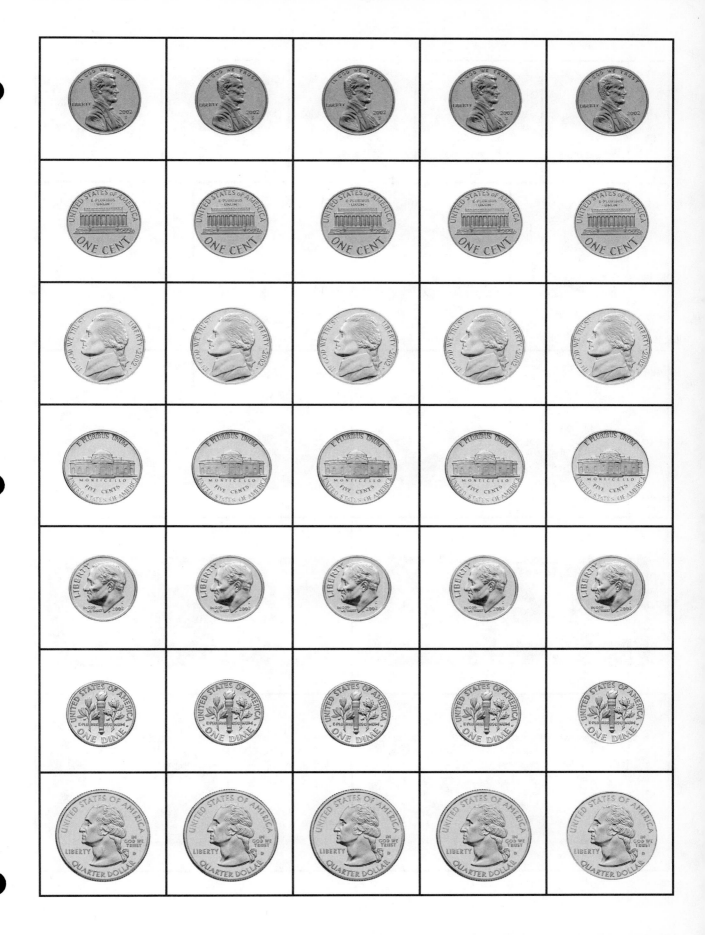

Coins and Bills

Bills

Bills

Bills

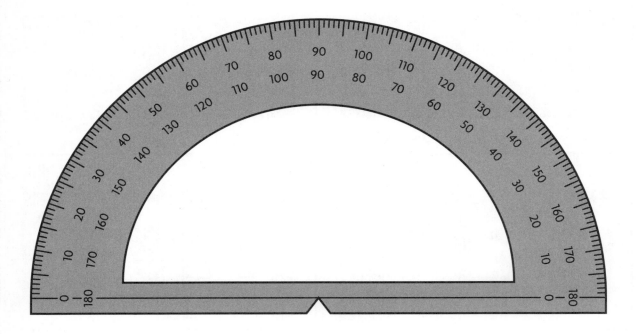

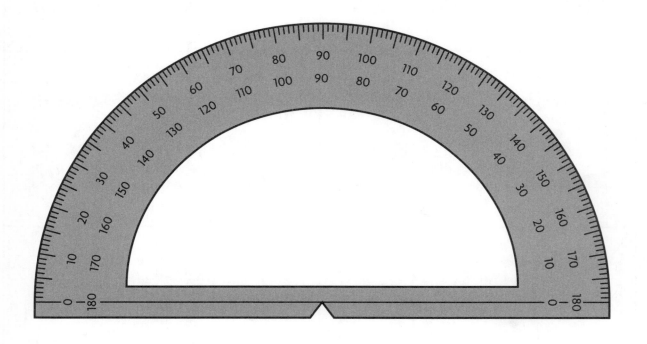

Protractors

inches

1 2 3 4 5 6 7 8 9

inches

1 2 3 4 5 6 7 8 9

cm
1 2 3 4 5 6 7 8 9 10 11 12 13 14 15 16 17 18 19 20 21 22

1 dm (decimeter)　2 dm

cm
1 2 3 4 5 6 7 8 9 10 11 12 13 14 15 16 17 18 19 20 21 22

1 dm (decimeter)　2 dm

Rulers

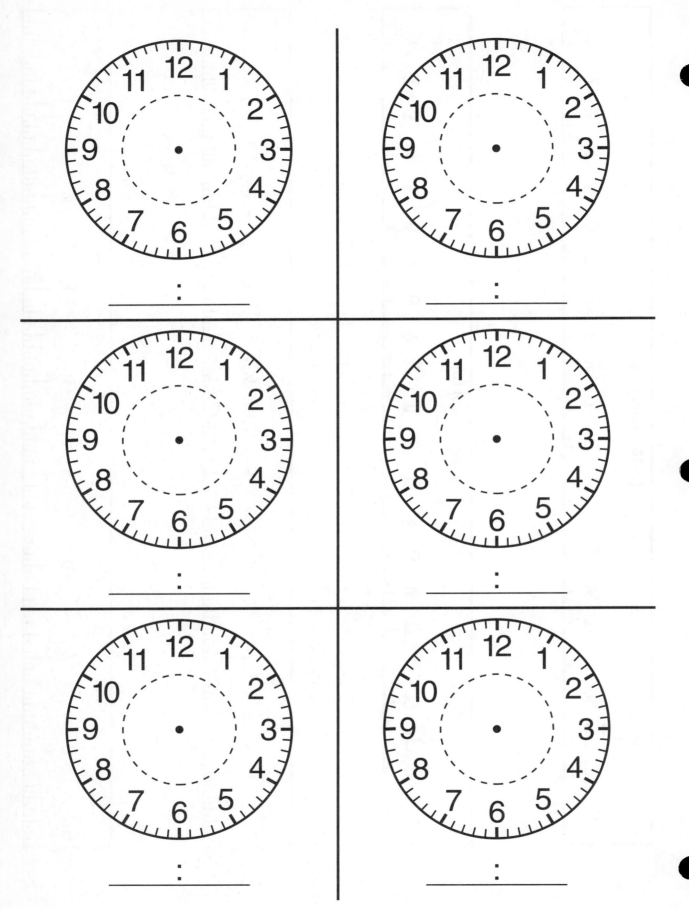

Analog Clockfaces

Sunday	Monday	Tuesday	Wednesday	Thursday	Friday	Saturday

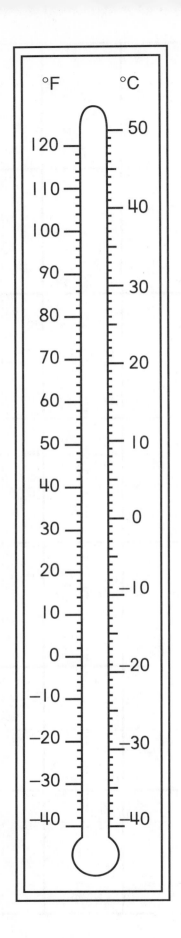

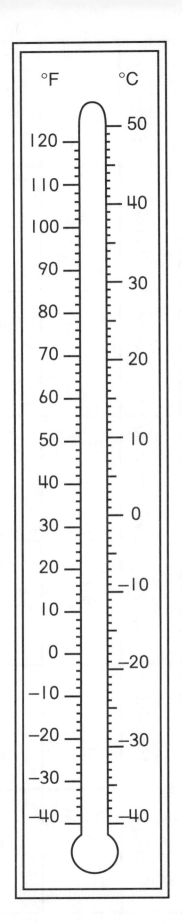

Thermometers (dual scale)

1-Inch Grid Paper

1-Centimeter Grid Paper

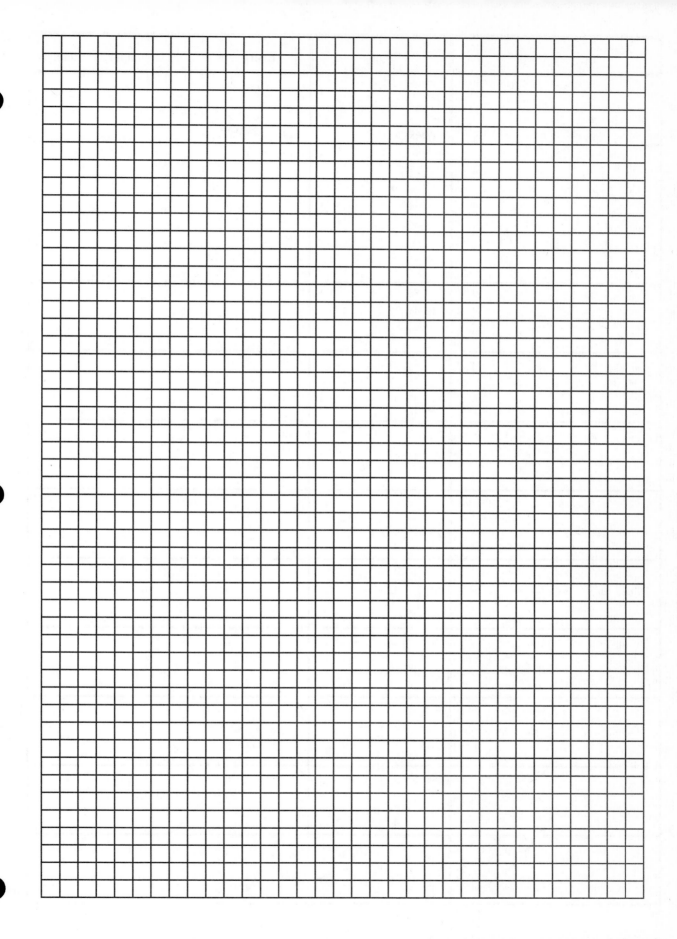

0.5-Centimeter Grid Paper

© Harcourt

	Tally	Frequency	Cumulative Frequency

Tally Table

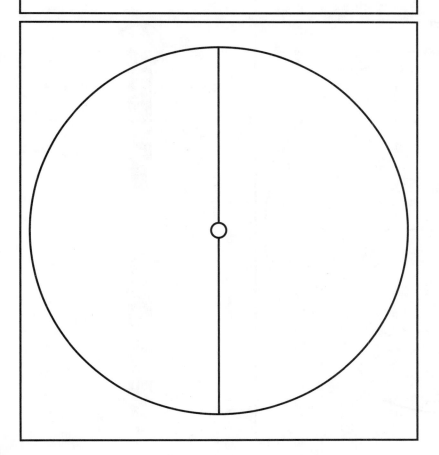

Spinner Tips

How to assemble spinner.
- Glue patterns to tagboard.
- Cut out and attach pointer with a fastener.

Alternative
- Students can use a paper clip and pencil instead.

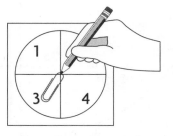

Spinners (blank and 2-section)

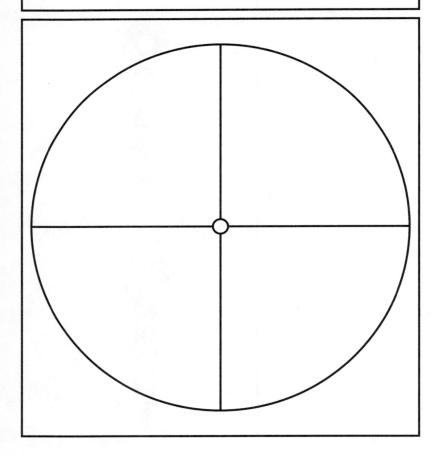

Spinner Tips

How to assemble spinner.
- Glue patterns to tagboard.
- Cut out and attach pointer with a fastener.

Alternative
- Students can use a paper clip and pencil instead.

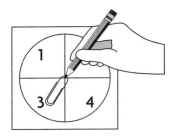

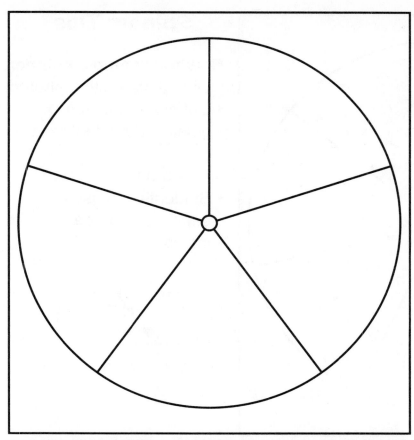

Spinner Tips

How to assemble spinner.
- Glue patterns to tagboard.
- Cut out and attach pointer with a fastener.

Alternative
- Students can use a paper clip and pencil instead.

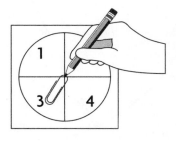

Spinners (5- and 6-section)

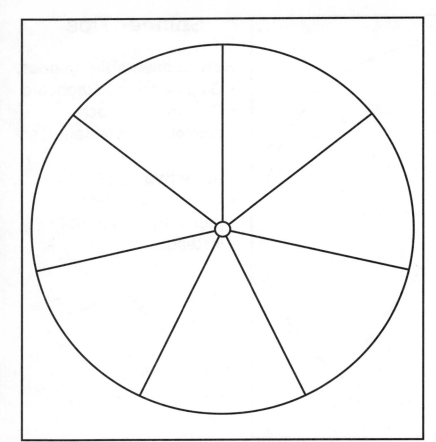

Spinner Tips

How to assemble spinner.
- Glue patterns to tagboard.
- Cut out and attach pointer with a fastener.

Alternative
- Students can use a paper clip and pencil instead.

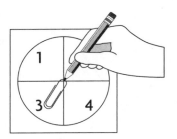

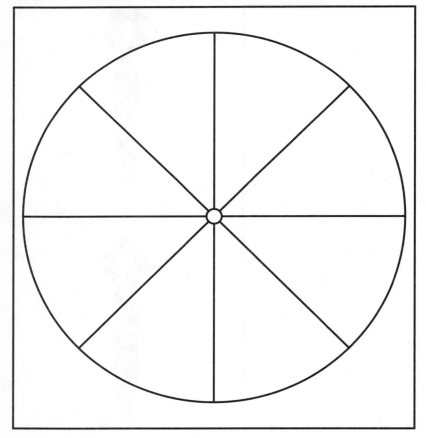

Spinners (7- and 8-section)

Spinner Tips

How to assemble spinner.
- Glue patterns to tagboard.
- Cut out and attach pointer with a fastener.

Alternative
- Students can use a paper clip and pencil instead.

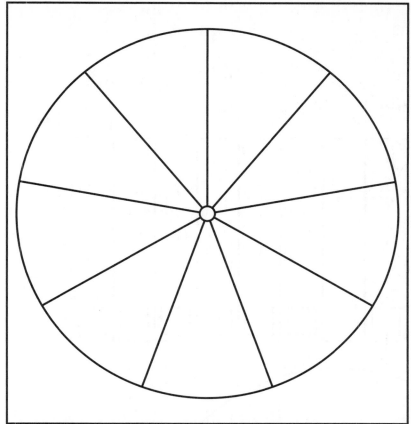

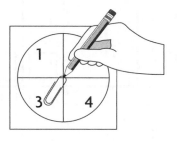

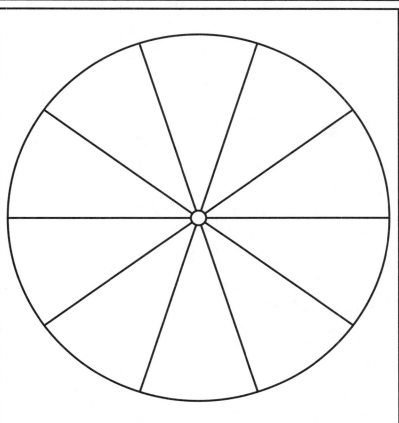

Spinners (9- and 10-section)

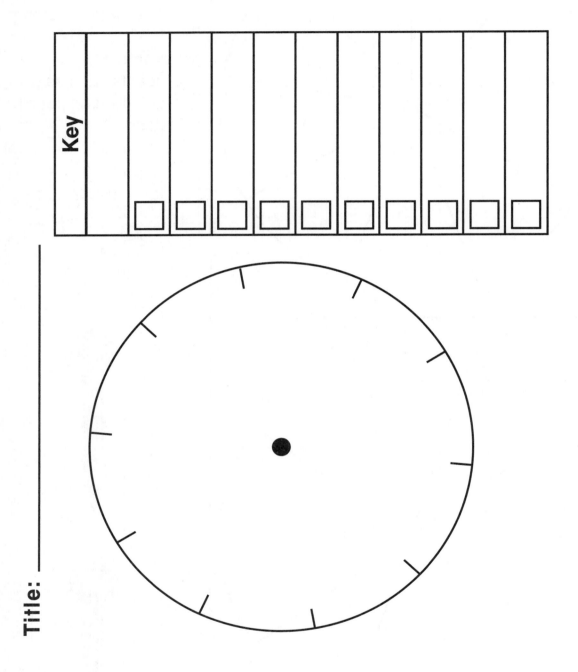

Key

Title: _____

Circle Graph Pattern (tenths)

© Harcourt

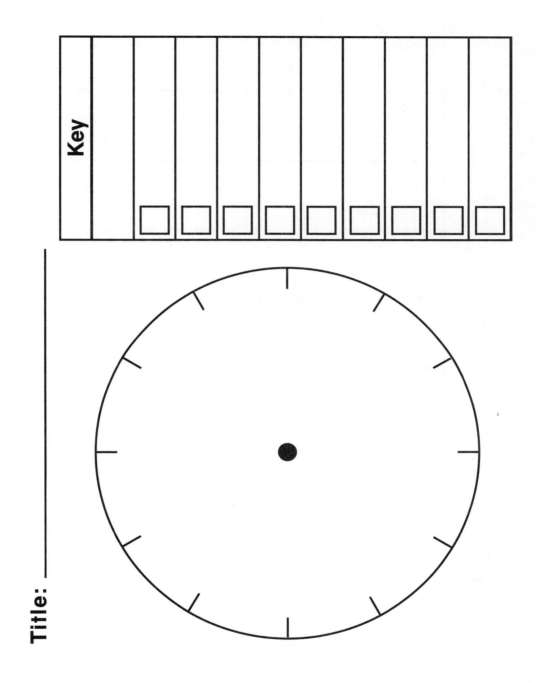

Key

Title: _____

Circle Graph Pattern (twelfths)

Title_____

0

Bar Graph/Histogram Pattern

Title_____

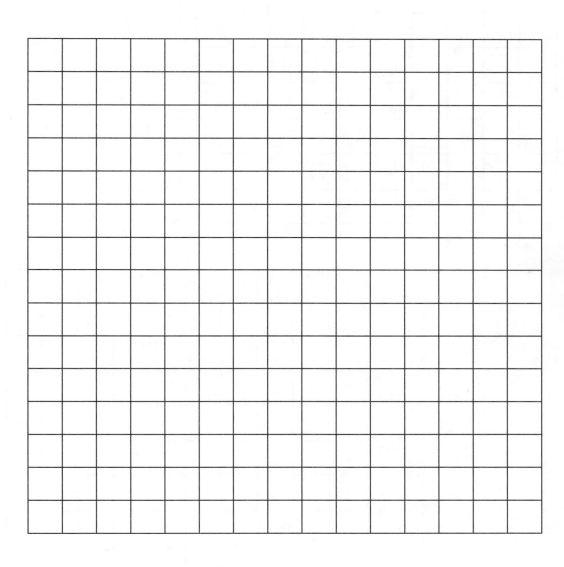

Line Graph Pattern

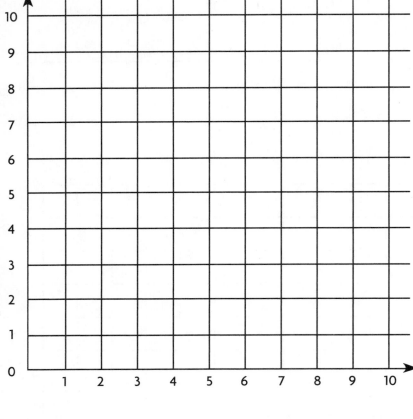

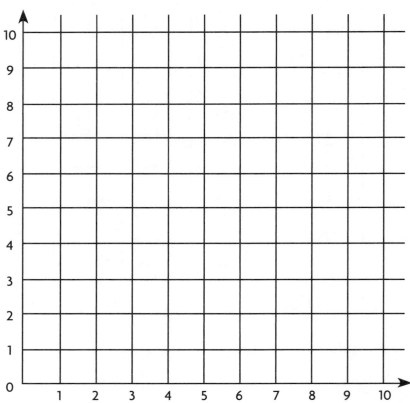

Grid of Quadrant 1

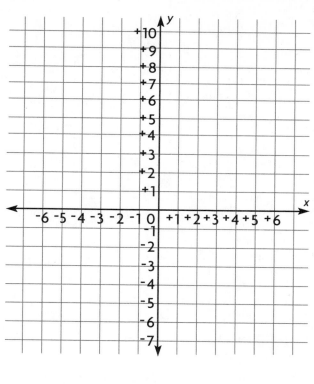
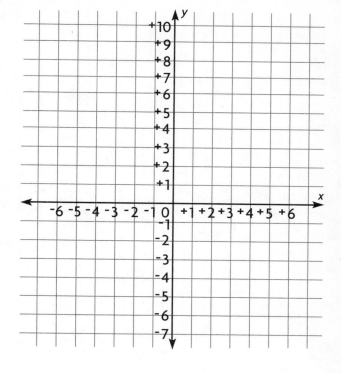
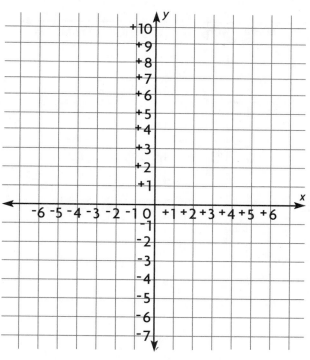
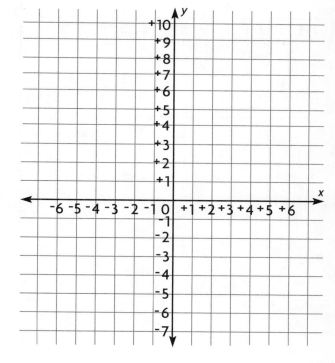

Coordinate Planes

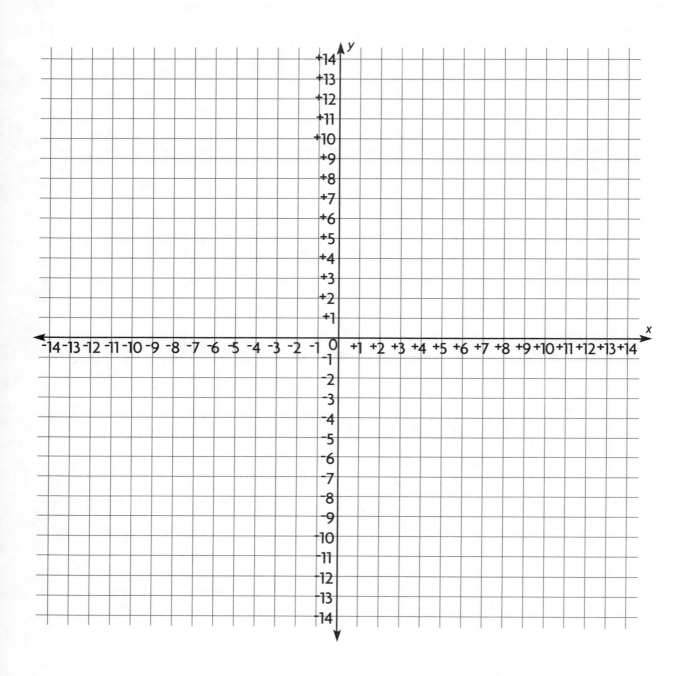

Large Coordinate Plane

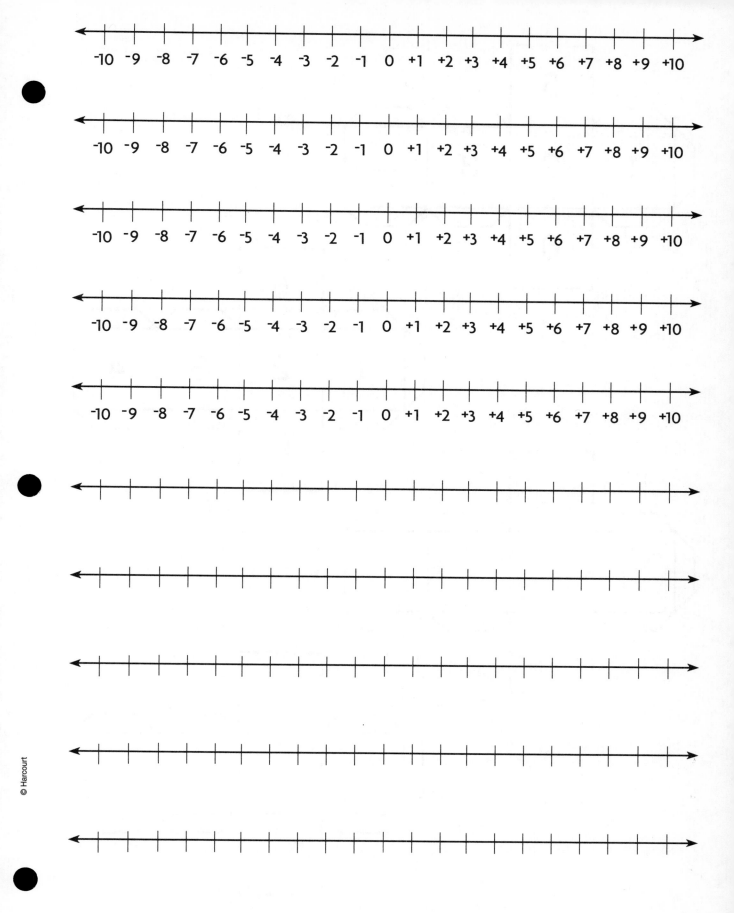

Number Lines (integers)

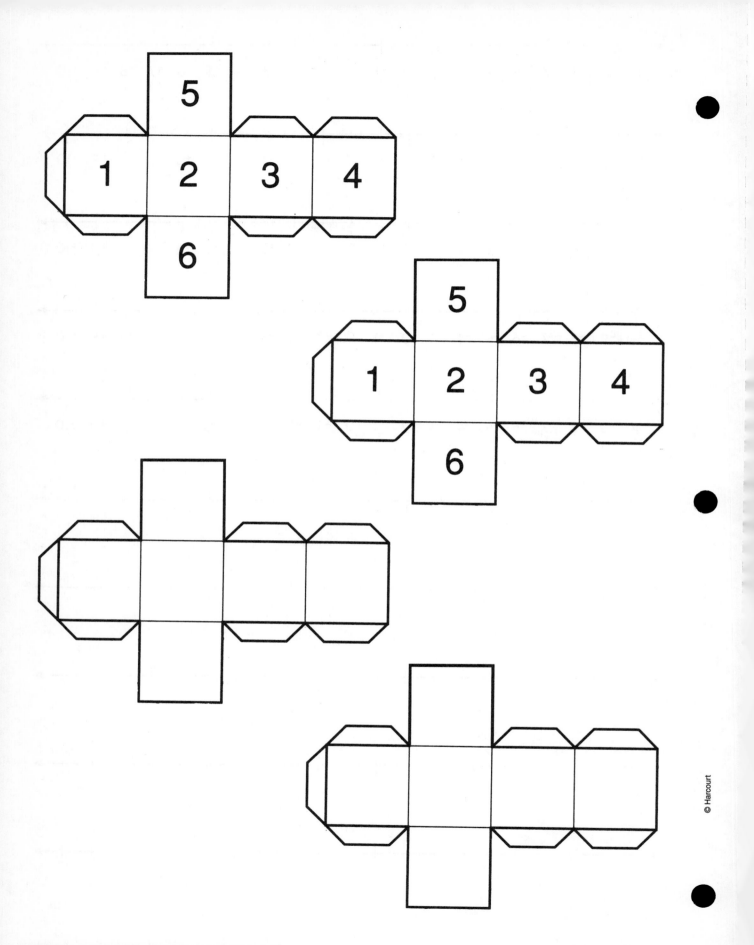

Number Cube Patterns

Dot Paper

Triangle Dot Paper

© Harcourt

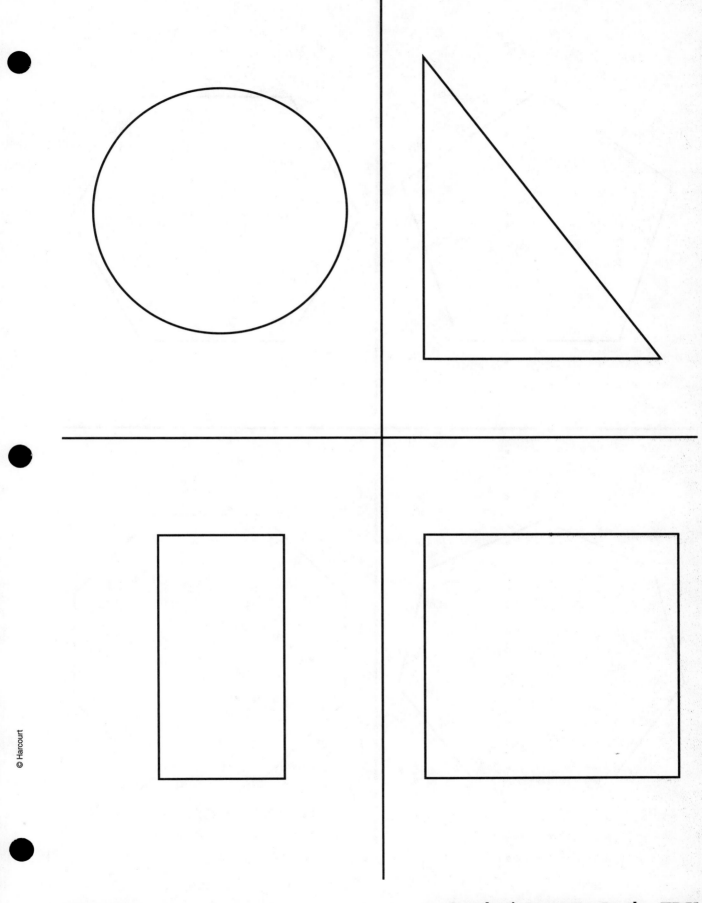

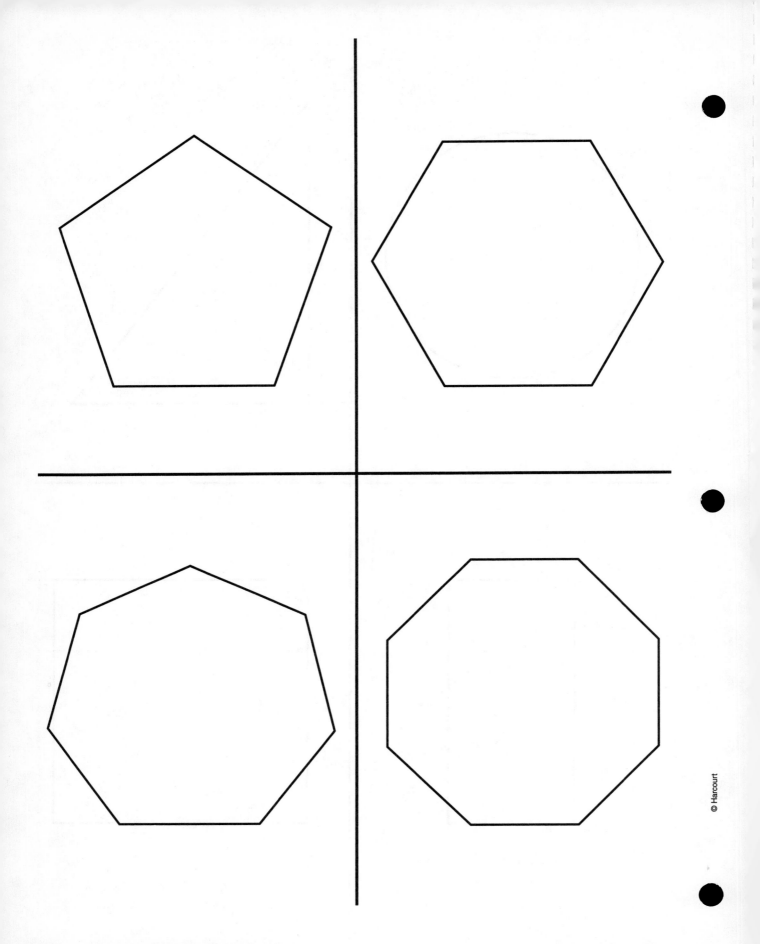

Polygons: Multi-Sided

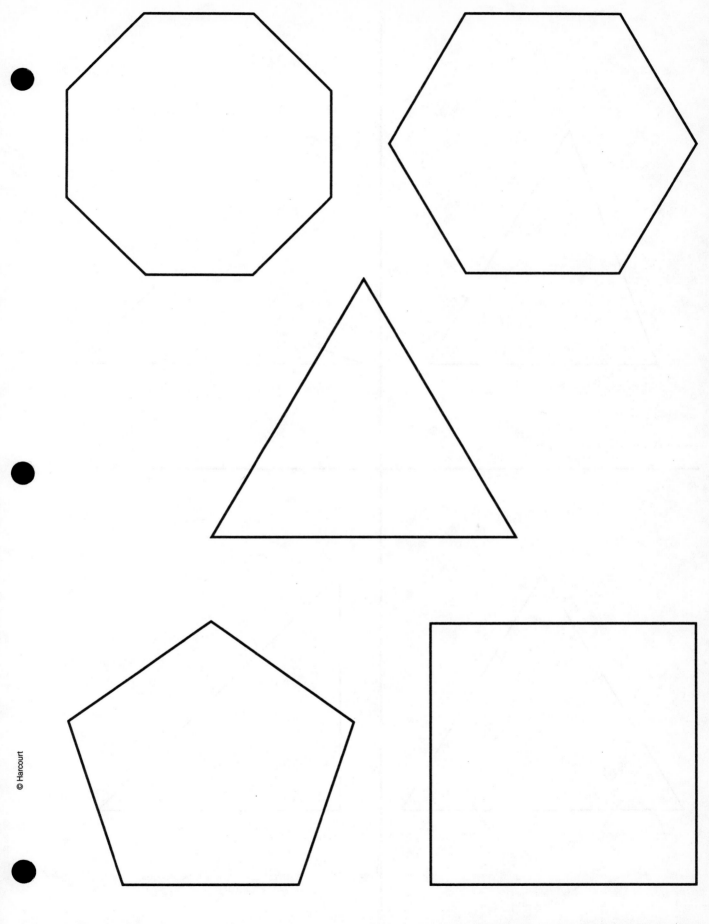

Regular Polygons

© Harcourt

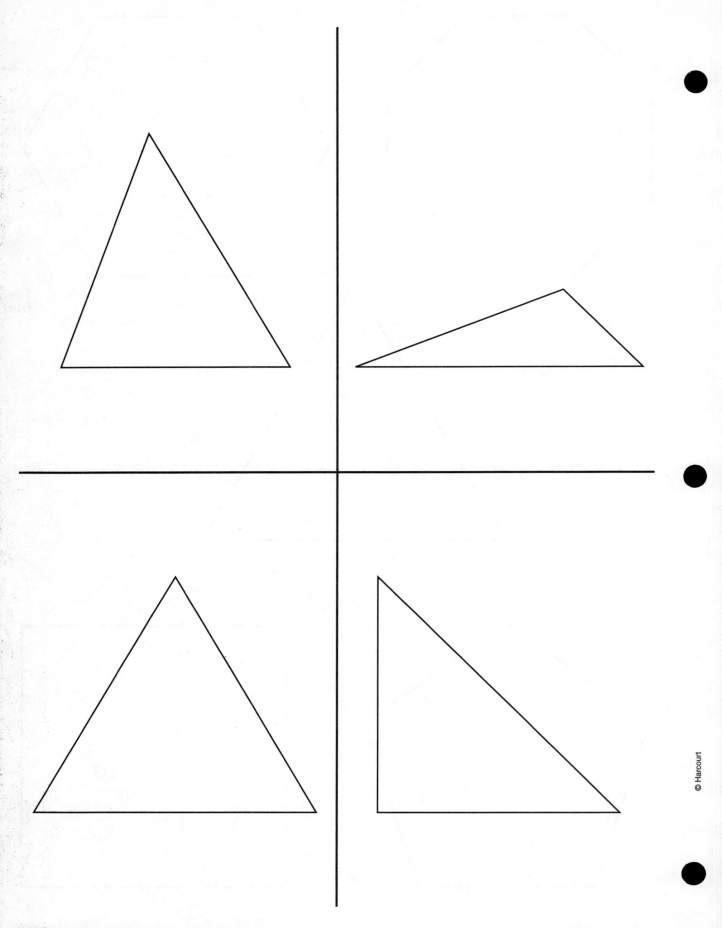

Polygons: Triangles

© Harcourt

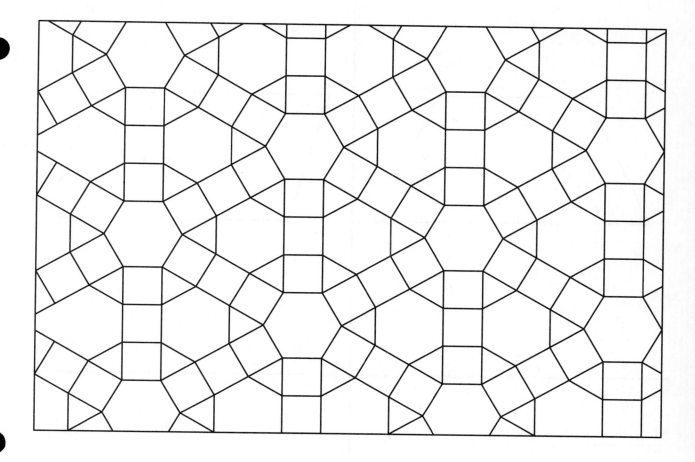

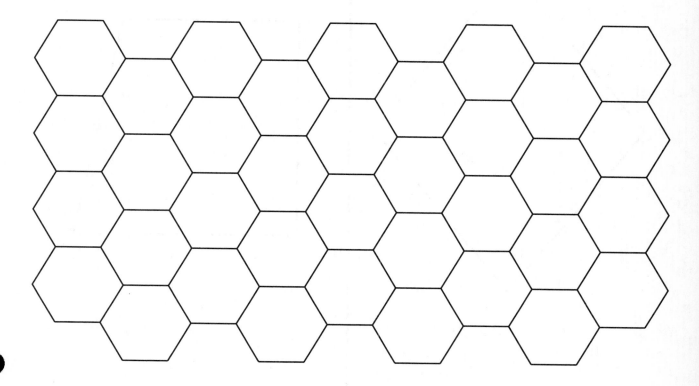

Tessellation Patterns

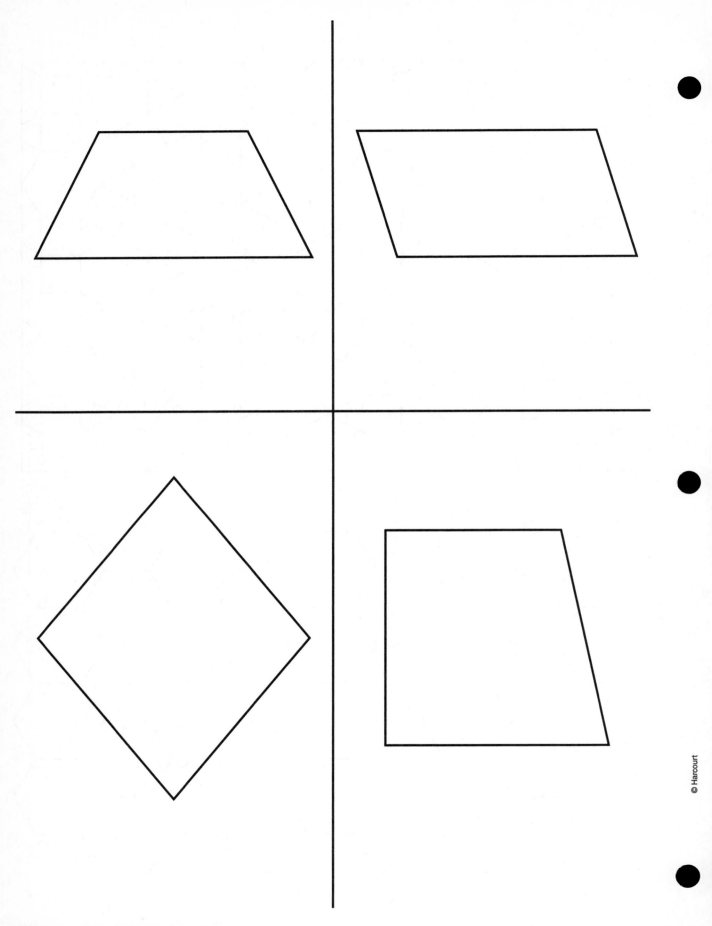

Polygons: Quadrilaterals

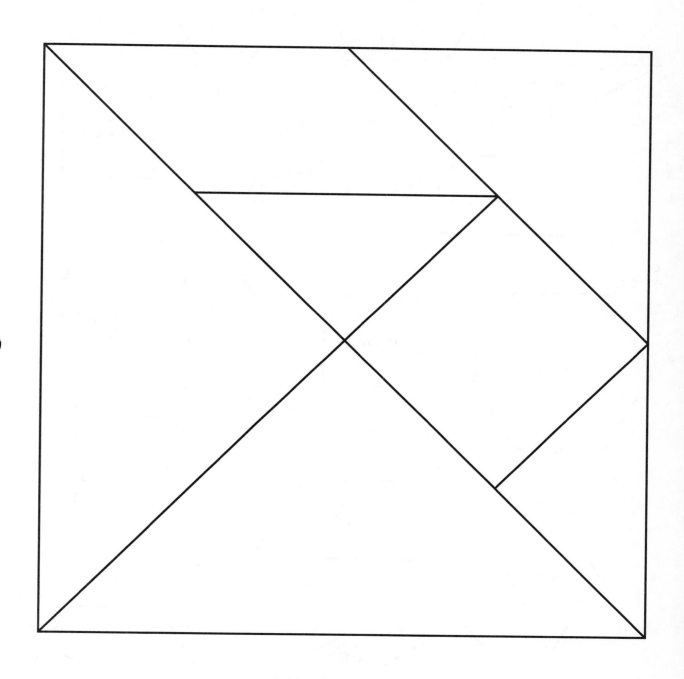

Tangram Pattern

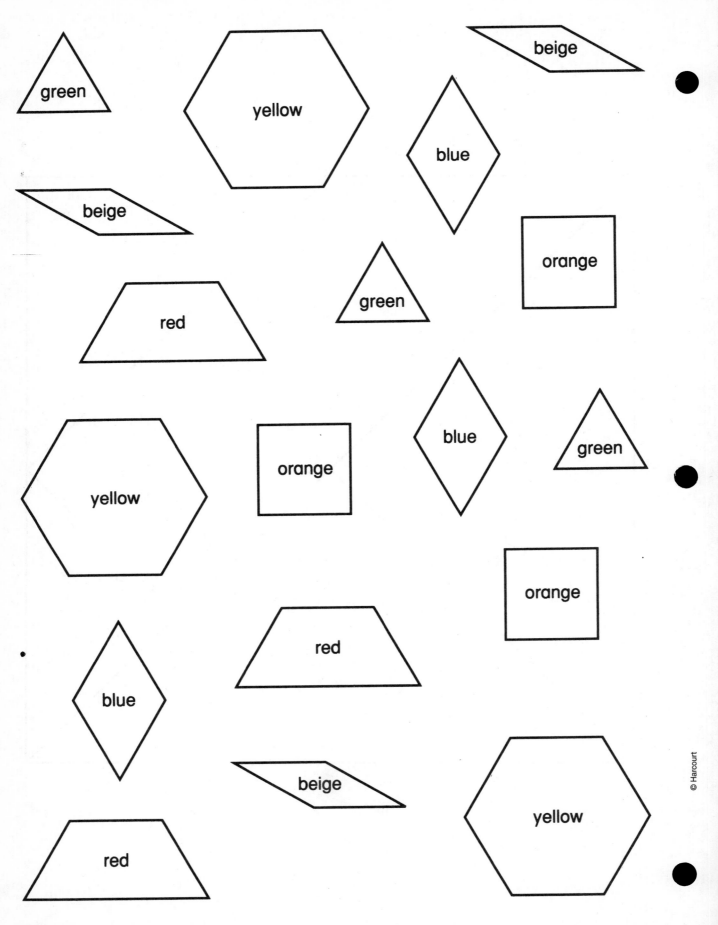

Pattern Block Patterns

© Harcourt

Circles

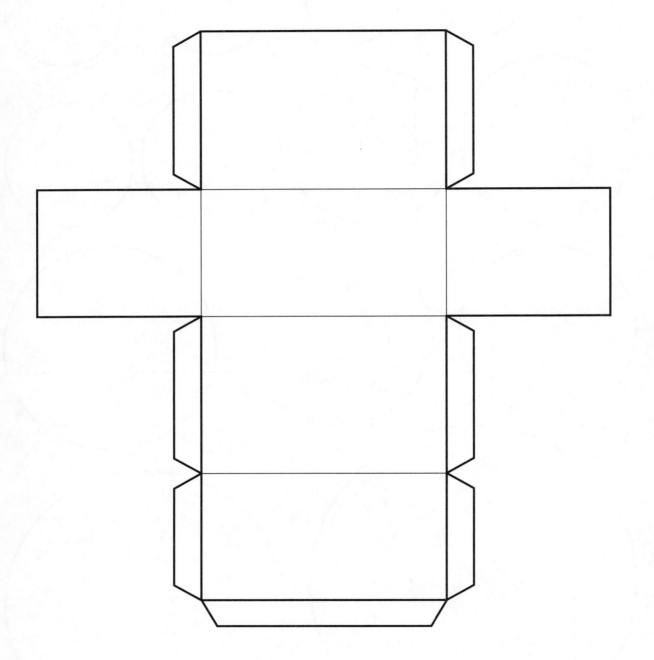

Rectangular Prism Pattern

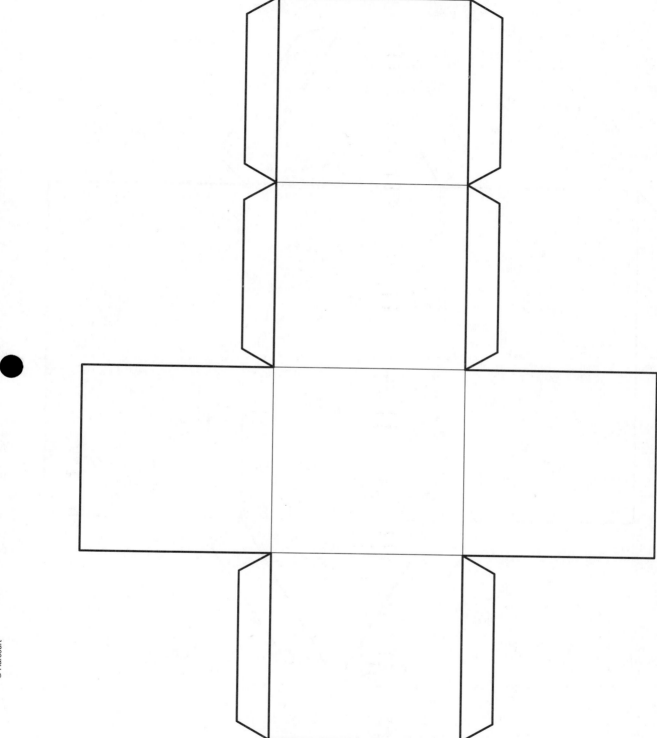

Cube Pattern

Triangular Prism Pattern

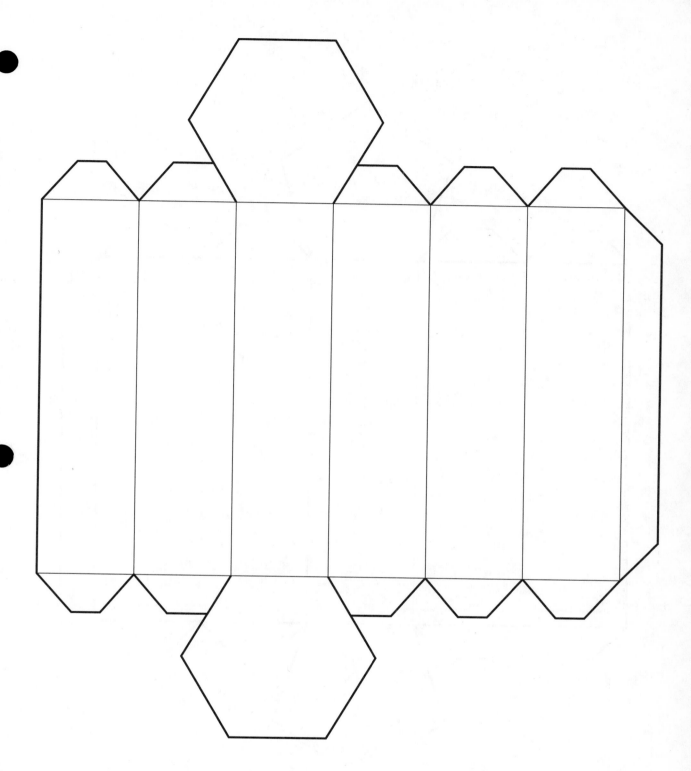

Hexagonal Prism Pattern

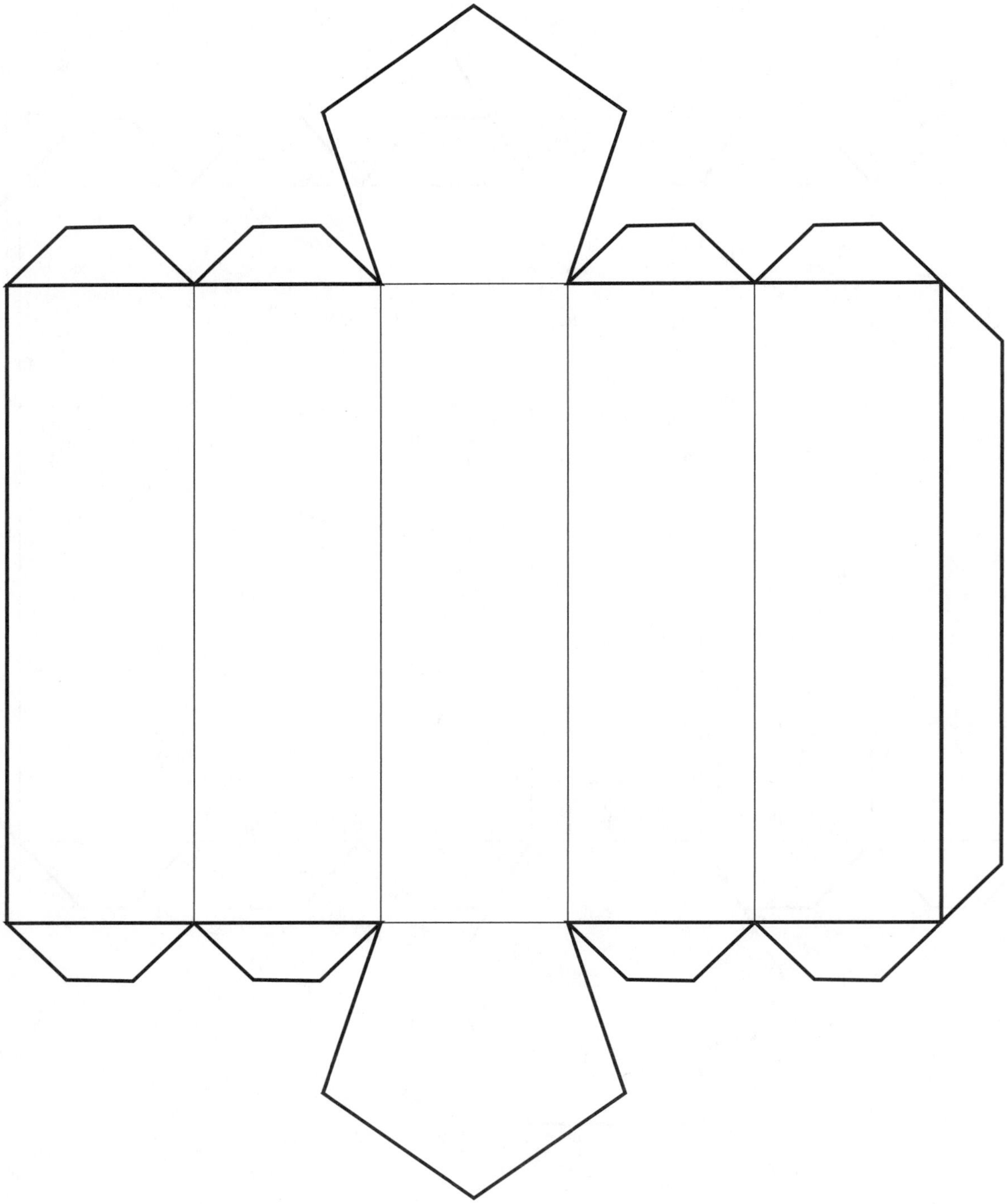

Teacher's Resource Book

Pentagonal Prism Pattern

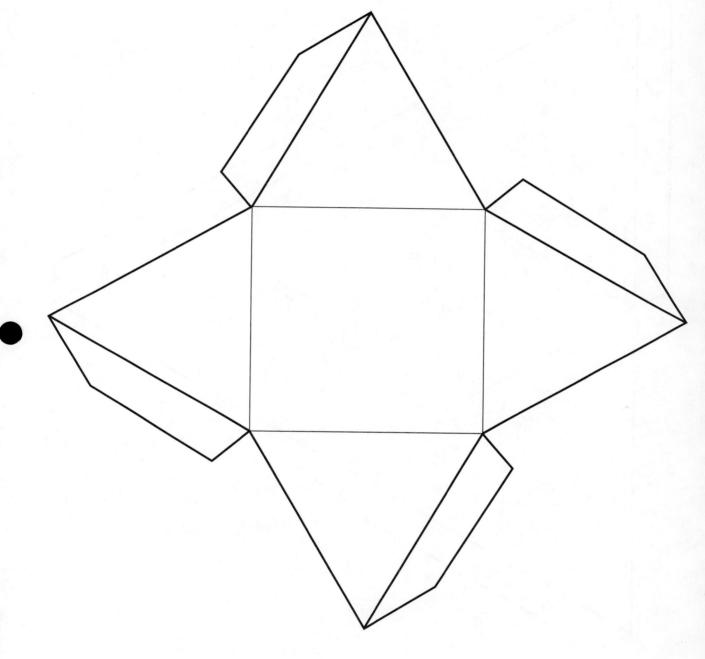

Square Pyramid Pattern

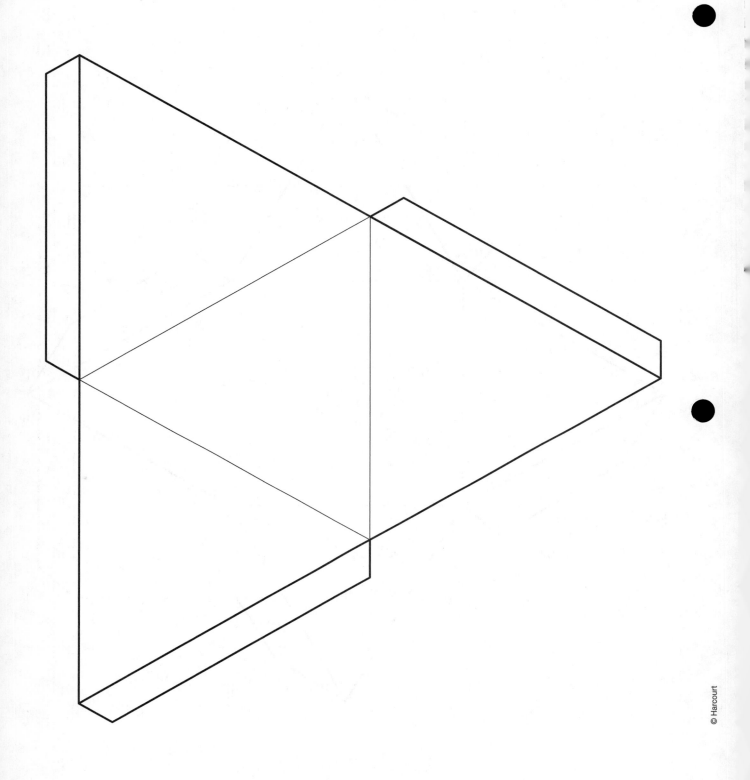

Triangular Pyramid Pattern

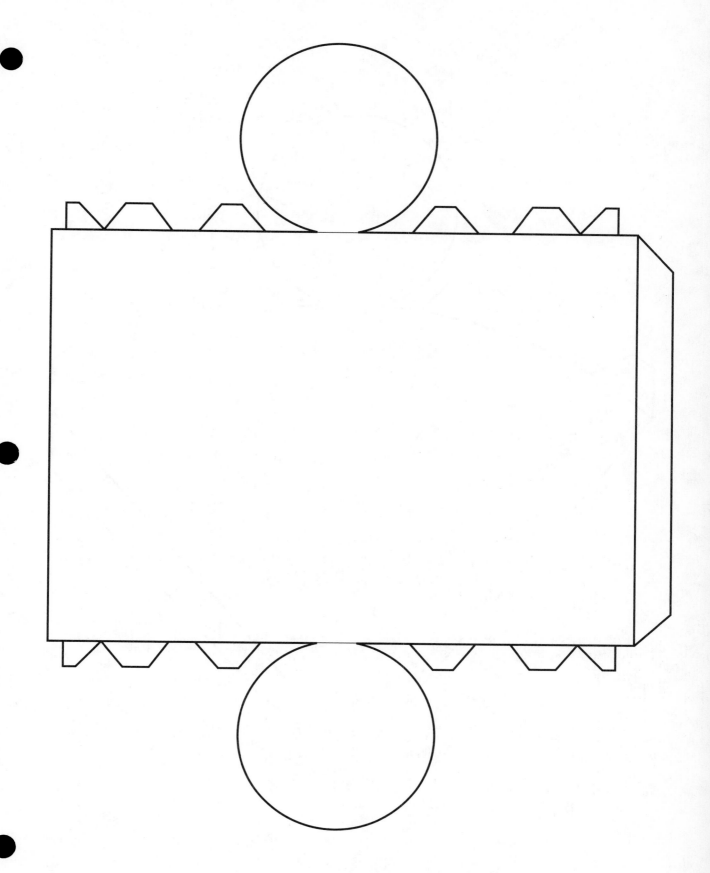

Cylinder Pattern

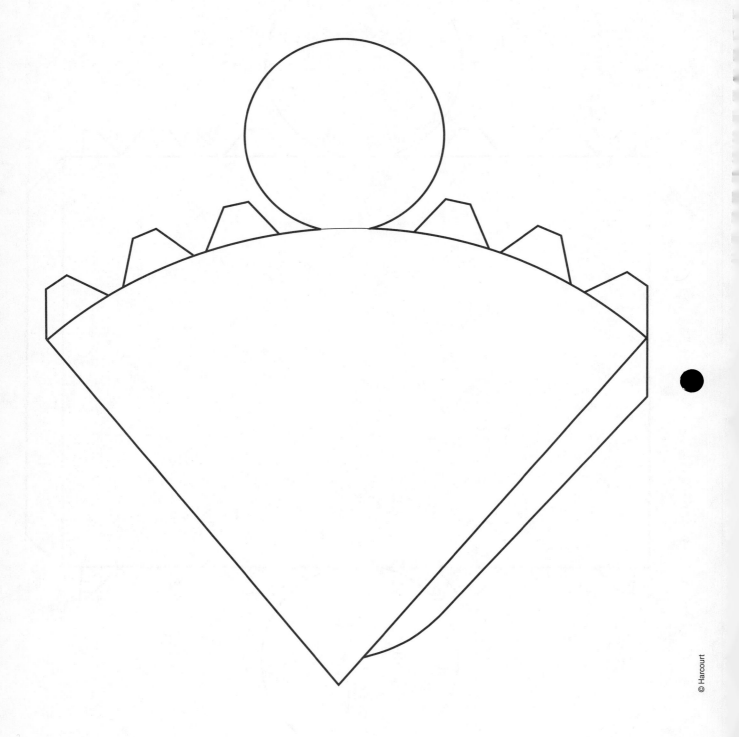

Cone Pattern

© Harcourt

Checking Account

Check Number	Date	Description	Amount of Check	Amount of Deposit	Balance

Checking Account

SILLY NUMBERS

© Harcourt

The number of letters in your last name	Your telephone area code
The number of letters in your teacher's last on name	The total number of toes on the left feet of the players of this game
The number of letters in the title of your favorite TV show	The first three digits of your telephone number
The number of stars on the American flag	The number of letters in the full name of your school
The number of letters in the full name of the person sitting to your left	The last three digits of your zip code

The number of letters in your first name	The total number of pockets on players' clothes
Last three digits of your telephone number	The number of boys in the room
The number of girls in the room	The total number of people in the room
The total number of pennies needed to buy lunch at school	The number the minute hand of a watch or clock is pointing to
The total number of fingers playing this game	The total number of chairs in the room

Silly Numbers

$5\overline{)4.5}$	$6\overline{)3.37}$	$4\overline{)4.59}$	$2\overline{)2.4}$	$9\overline{)3.7}$
$8\overline{)8.84}$	$5\overline{)2.07}$	$6\overline{)36.6}$	$2\overline{)19.5}$	$9\overline{)36.9}$
$7\overline{)63.7}$	$7\overline{)3.51}$	$3\overline{)27.9}$	$5\overline{)3.55}$	$4\overline{)3.28}$
$8\overline{)532}$	$9\overline{)264}$	$8\overline{)695}$	$7\overline{)216}$	$8\overline{)139}$
$4\overline{)364}$	$3\overline{)176}$	$9\overline{)476}$	$2\overline{)0.64}$	$3\overline{)0.79}$
$5\overline{)4.55}$	$4\overline{)2.44}$	$3\overline{)0.396}$	$7\overline{)894}$	$4\overline{)379}$
$9\overline{)173}$	$2\overline{)843}$	$3\overline{)0.874}$	$6\overline{)0.489}$	$5\overline{)0.719}$
$8\overline{)0.459}$	$2\overline{)8.62}$	$7\overline{)0.597}$	$4\overline{)0.895}$	$8\overline{)0.589}$

Predict and Test

Round 1

Possible Outcomes	Color	Color	Color
Predicted Frequency			
Actual Frequency			

Round 2

Possible Outcomes	Color	Color	Color
Predicted Frequency			
Actual Frequency			

Round 3

Possible Outcomes	Color	Color	Color
Predicted Frequency			
Actual Frequency			

Predictions

Triangle

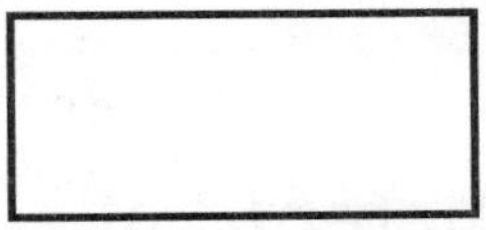

Rectangle

Square

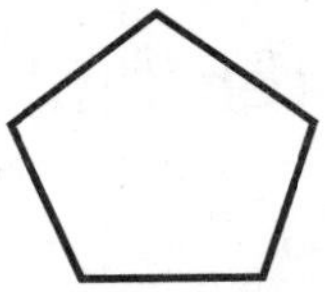

Pentagon

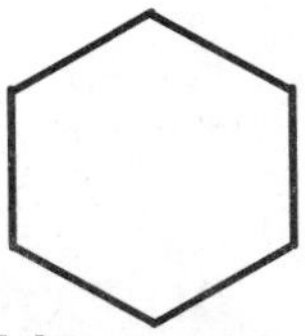

Hexagon

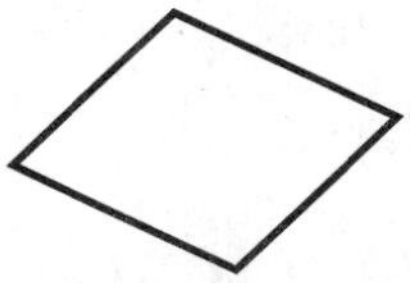

Rhombus

Translation

Rotation

Reflection

Translation

Rotation

Reflection

Transformations

centimeter (cm)	unit of length
decimeter (dm)	unit of length
kilometer (km)	unit of length
meter (m)	unit of length
millimeter (mm)	unit of length
gram (g)	unit of mass
kilogram (kg)	unit of mass
milligram (mg)	unit of mass
milliliter (mL)	unit of capacity
liter (L)	unit of capacity

BINGO

		FREE		

Math Award

To _____

For _____

_____

_____

By _____

EXCELLENCE

On this day of _____

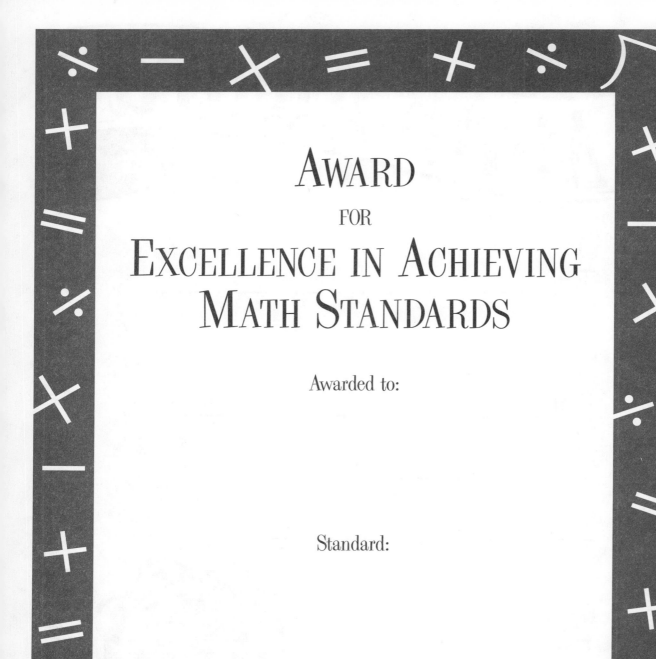

AWARD

FOR

EXCELLENCE IN ACHIEVING MATH STANDARDS

Awarded to:

Standard:

Signed _____

Date _____

Daily Facts Practice

A	10 +3	4 +6	2 +5	2 +7	6 +6	8 +4
B	10 +10	3 +4	8 +1	3 +9	0 +4	7 +3
C	6 −5	13 −3	12 −7	18 −9	14 −8	11 −2
D	16 −10	13 −9	9 −6	12 −4	7 −2	10 −5
E	9 +2	4 +5	8 +8	10 −3	9 −5	11 −9
F	5 ×6	12 ×2	4 ×0	12 ×8	7 ×5	3 ×7
G	2 ×10	4 ×9	11 ×4	5 ×3	7 ×6	3 ×12

Daily Facts Practice

A	$3\overline{)24}$	$2\overline{)10}$	$5\overline{)40}$	$5\overline{)55}$	$8\overline{)48}$	$6\overline{)32}$
B	$9\overline{)36}$	$7\overline{)21}$	$4\overline{)44}$	$\begin{array}{r}12\\ \times3\\ \hline\end{array}$	$\begin{array}{r}2\\ \times4\\ \hline\end{array}$	$\begin{array}{r}7\\ \times7\\ \hline\end{array}$
C	$\begin{array}{r}4\\ \times5\\ \hline\end{array}$	$\begin{array}{r}8\\ \times4\\ \hline\end{array}$	$\begin{array}{r}7\\ \times9\\ \hline\end{array}$	$12\overline{)36}$	$10\overline{)20}$	$7\overline{)56}$
D	$\begin{array}{r}1\\ +8\\ \hline\end{array}$	$\begin{array}{r}7\\ +9\\ \hline\end{array}$	$\begin{array}{r}5\\ +4\\ \hline\end{array}$	$\begin{array}{r}9\\ +3\\ \hline\end{array}$	$\begin{array}{r}4\\ +2\\ \hline\end{array}$	$\begin{array}{r}7\\ +7\\ \hline\end{array}$
E	$\begin{array}{r}9\\ +10\\ \hline\end{array}$	$\begin{array}{r}17\\ -8\\ \hline\end{array}$	$\begin{array}{r}5\\ +8\\ \hline\end{array}$	$\begin{array}{r}9\\ -7\\ \hline\end{array}$	$\begin{array}{r}9\\ +5\\ \hline\end{array}$	$\begin{array}{r}12\\ -6\\ \hline\end{array}$
F	$\begin{array}{r}17\\ -7\\ \hline\end{array}$	$\begin{array}{r}4\\ +8\\ \hline\end{array}$	$\begin{array}{r}9\\ -4\\ \hline\end{array}$	$\begin{array}{r}6\\ +8\\ \hline\end{array}$	$\begin{array}{r}8\\ -3\\ \hline\end{array}$	$\begin{array}{r}3\\ +5\\ \hline\end{array}$
G	$\begin{array}{r}10\\ -2\\ \hline\end{array}$	$\begin{array}{r}7\\ +6\\ \hline\end{array}$	$\begin{array}{r}5\\ +2\\ \hline\end{array}$	$\begin{array}{r}8\\ +3\\ \hline\end{array}$	$\begin{array}{r}8\\ -6\\ \hline\end{array}$	$\begin{array}{r}16\\ -7\\ \hline\end{array}$

Daily Facts Practice

A	11 −1	9 −3	5 −4	12 −8	11 −4	14 −5
B	2 +9	8 +7	9 +0	7 +4	6 +2	4 +7
C	8 +9	17 −9	13 −5	11 −7	14 −4	4 +10
D	16 −8	8 +5	9 +9	2 +6	6 +7	9 −2
E	10 −6	13 −4	5 −3	8 −5	14 −10	13 −6
F	2 +8	11 −3	8 +6	10 +7	15 −9	4 −2
G	11 ×10	6 ×4	8 ×2	6 ×12	9 ×8	5 ×1

Daily Facts Practice

A	9 +8	3 +3	8 +2	5 +6	6 +4	3 +6
B	4 +4	1 +10	5 +9	3 +2	10 +5	9 +7
C	0 +7	6 +5	5 +3	7 +2	4 +9	3 +8
D	4 +3	8 −7	7 +5	10 −4	11 −8	9 +6
E	6 ×3	9 ×5	4 ×7	6 ×8	11 ×9	3 ×4
F	10 ×12	6 ×6	9 ×7	7 ×2	4 ×8	2 ×9
G	6 ×5	12 ×7	5 ×9	7 ×10	11 ×11	8 ×6

Daily Facts Practice

A	12 $\times 5$	$10\overline{)120}$	7 $\times 4$	$9\overline{)18}$	6 $\times 11$	$5\overline{)45}$
B	16 -9	6 -4	8 -1	12 -5	13 -7	14 -9
C	18 -10	13 -8	6 -3	15 -6	14 -7	11 -6
D	5 -2	7 -4	12 -9	15 -7	7 -5	14 -6
E	6 $+9$	17 -10	2 $+3$	12 -3	9 $+4$	10 -7
F	1 $+4$	7 $+8$	6 $+3$	5 $+7$	10 $+8$	4 $+5$
G	3 $+7$	2 $+4$	9 $+5$	6 $+10$	3 $+8$	7 $+4$

Daily Facts Practice

A	2 +2	6 +9	7 −3	6 +6	8 −4	15 −8
B	10 −8	6 −2	2 +10	6 +7	5 +3	7 −3
C	4 −3	10 −4	13 −5	6 +2	9 +9	5 +1
D	12 −10	11 −2	6 −2	10 −7	13 −6	10 −8
E	14 −6	10 −1	12 −7	17 −8	15 −9	10 −5
F	5 ×4	6 ×9	6)‾48	8)‾64	6 ×7	12 ×4
G	2 ×7	8 ×12	9 ×3	4 ×2	8 ×8	12 ×6

Daily Facts Practice

A	$\begin{array}{r} 3 \\ \times 2 \\ \hline \end{array}$	$\begin{array}{r} 7 \\ \times 3 \\ \hline \end{array}$	$\begin{array}{r} 12 \\ \times 12 \\ \hline \end{array}$	$\begin{array}{r} 8 \\ \times 9 \\ \hline \end{array}$	$\begin{array}{r} 4 \\ \times 6 \\ \hline \end{array}$	$\begin{array}{r} 5 \\ \times 5 \\ \hline \end{array}$
B	$\begin{array}{r} 8 \\ \times 3 \\ \hline \end{array}$	$\begin{array}{r} 9 \\ \times 6 \\ \hline \end{array}$	$\begin{array}{r} 5 \\ \times 7 \\ \hline \end{array}$	$\begin{array}{r} 11 \\ \times 12 \\ \hline \end{array}$	$\begin{array}{r} 7 \\ \times 8 \\ \hline \end{array}$	$\begin{array}{r} 3 \\ \times 6 \\ \hline \end{array}$
C	$\begin{array}{r} 11 \\ \times 7 \\ \hline \end{array}$	$\begin{array}{r} 8 \\ \times 5 \\ \hline \end{array}$	$12\overline{)84}$	$\begin{array}{r} 8 \\ \times 7 \\ \hline \end{array}$	$9\overline{)54}$	$7\overline{)49}$
D	$\begin{array}{r} 0 \\ \times 3 \\ \hline \end{array}$	$\begin{array}{r} 4 \\ \times 4 \\ \hline \end{array}$	$\begin{array}{r} 5 \\ \times 8 \\ \hline \end{array}$	$\begin{array}{r} 3 \\ \times 5 \\ \hline \end{array}$	$\begin{array}{r} 7 \\ \times 12 \\ \hline \end{array}$	$\begin{array}{r} 9 \\ \times 9 \\ \hline \end{array}$
E	$4\overline{)24}$	$9\overline{)99}$	$\begin{array}{r} 9 \\ \times 4 \\ \hline \end{array}$	$4\overline{)32}$	$8\overline{)56}$	$\begin{array}{r} 4 \\ \times 12 \\ \hline \end{array}$
F	$\begin{array}{r} 5 \\ \times 12 \\ \hline \end{array}$	$\begin{array}{r} 3 \\ \times 8 \\ \hline \end{array}$	$\begin{array}{r} 10 \\ \times 7 \\ \hline \end{array}$	$\begin{array}{r} 3 \\ \times 9 \\ \hline \end{array}$	$\begin{array}{r} 6 \\ \times 5 \\ \hline \end{array}$	$\begin{array}{r} 9 \\ \times 12 \\ \hline \end{array}$
G	$\begin{array}{r} 12 \\ \times 11 \\ \hline \end{array}$	$\begin{array}{r} 3 \\ \times 3 \\ \hline \end{array}$	$\begin{array}{r} 9 \\ \times 4 \\ \hline \end{array}$	$\begin{array}{r} 3 \\ \times 10 \\ \hline \end{array}$	$\begin{array}{r} 2 \\ \times 6 \\ \hline \end{array}$	$\begin{array}{r} 7 \\ \times 6 \\ \hline \end{array}$

Daily Facts Practice

A	8 ×11	9 ×7	4 ×3	3 ×8	6 ×9	4 ×12
B	10 ×3	9 ×2	12 ×4	9)27	5)30	4)16
C	6)0	12)108	6)18	7 ×7	5 ×2	11 ×6
D	3)15	11)110	9)63	4)36	8)72	12)144
E	8)96	7)7	4)28	9)45	10)60	7)63
F	6)54	4)12	5)60	7)28	12)96	8)32
G	6 ×2	6)36	3)21	8 ×3	12)72	9)81

Daily Facts Practice

A	$\begin{array}{r} 0 \\ \times 5 \\ \hline \end{array}$	$6\overline{)42}$	$\begin{array}{r} 7 \\ \times 8 \\ \hline \end{array}$	$12\overline{)132}$	$\begin{array}{r} 4 \\ \times 11 \\ \hline \end{array}$ $11\overline{)55}$
B	$7\overline{)35}$	$12\overline{)48}$	$3\overline{)27}$	$2\overline{)16}$	$8\overline{)40}$ $10\overline{)100}$
C	$4\overline{)20}$	$7\overline{)42}$	$6\overline{)24}$	$9\overline{)72}$	$11\overline{)121}$ $8\overline{)24}$
D	$6\overline{)60}$	$5\overline{)35}$	$12\overline{)60}$	$3\overline{)18}$	$7\overline{)84}$ $5\overline{)15}$
E	$9\overline{)108}$	$11\overline{)132}$	$\begin{array}{r} 12 \\ \times 9 \\ \hline \end{array}$	$9\overline{)27}$	$6\overline{)48}$ $\begin{array}{r} 2 \\ \times 8 \\ \hline \end{array}$
F	$6\overline{)72}$	$3\overline{)9}$	$5\overline{)25}$	$7\overline{)77}$	$10\overline{)110}$ $12\overline{)24}$
G	$\begin{array}{r} 11 \\ \times 2 \\ \hline \end{array}$	$\begin{array}{r} 10 \\ \times 5 \\ \hline \end{array}$	$\begin{array}{r} 6 \\ \times 4 \\ \hline \end{array}$	$\begin{array}{r} 8 \\ \times 8 \\ \hline \end{array}$	$2\overline{)14}$ $8\overline{)56}$

Daily Facts Practice

A	$\begin{array}{r} 0 \\ \times 9 \\ \hline \end{array}$	$3\overline{)36}$	$\begin{array}{r} 7 \\ \times 12 \\ \hline \end{array}$	$9\overline{)0}$	$\begin{array}{r} 9 \\ \times 11 \\ \hline \end{array}$	$4\overline{)28}$
B	$12\overline{)84}$	$9\overline{)63}$	$3\overline{)30}$	$5\overline{)10}$	$7\overline{)49}$	$6\overline{)32}$
C	$12\overline{)120}$	$8\overline{)16}$	$3\overline{)24}$	$2\overline{)20}$	$7\overline{)28}$	$5\overline{)20}$
D	$11\overline{)121}$	$\begin{array}{r} 2 \\ \times 5 \\ \hline \end{array}$	$\begin{array}{r} 9 \\ \times 6 \\ \hline \end{array}$	$\begin{array}{r} 6 \\ \times 3 \\ \hline \end{array}$	$\begin{array}{r} 8 \\ \times 5 \\ \hline \end{array}$	$9\overline{)90}$
E	$3\overline{)12}$	$8\overline{)48}$	$12\overline{)96}$	$5\overline{)0}$	$7\overline{)14}$	$2\overline{)18}$
F	$\begin{array}{r} 4 \\ \times 7 \\ \hline \end{array}$	$11\overline{)88}$	$5\overline{)35}$	$7\overline{)84}$	$6\overline{)12}$	$\begin{array}{r} 7 \\ \times 4 \\ \hline \end{array}$
G	$12\overline{)12}$	$1\overline{)9}$	$4\overline{)48}$	$6\overline{)36}$	$12\overline{)0}$	$7\overline{)63}$

Daily Facts Practice

A	$2\overline{)6}$	$9\overline{)9}$	$8\overline{)32}$	$12\overline{)36}$	$5\overline{)20}$	$3\overline{)33}$

B	$7\overline{)70}$	$\begin{array}{r}4\\\times5\\\hline\end{array}$	$5\overline{)45}$	$\begin{array}{r}12\\\times7\\\hline\end{array}$	$4\overline{)36}$	$\begin{array}{r}9\\\times9\\\hline\end{array}$

C	$10\overline{)50}$	$4\overline{)16}$	$2\overline{)22}$	$9\overline{)72}$	$3\overline{)18}$	$7\overline{)42}$

D	$\begin{array}{r}2\\\times12\\\hline\end{array}$	$\begin{array}{r}9\\\times5\\\hline\end{array}$	$\begin{array}{r}0\\\times6\\\hline\end{array}$	$\begin{array}{r}4\\\times8\\\hline\end{array}$	$\begin{array}{r}10\\\times10\\\hline\end{array}$	$\begin{array}{r}5\\\times7\\\hline\end{array}$

E	$\begin{array}{r}4\\+6\\\hline\end{array}$	$\begin{array}{r}9\\+7\\\hline\end{array}$	$\begin{array}{r}10\\+2\\\hline\end{array}$	$\begin{array}{r}8\\+3\\\hline\end{array}$	$\begin{array}{r}3\\+3\\\hline\end{array}$	$\begin{array}{r}4\\+9\\\hline\end{array}$

F	$\begin{array}{r}10\\+4\\\hline\end{array}$	$\begin{array}{r}11\\-9\\\hline\end{array}$	$\begin{array}{r}8\\+5\\\hline\end{array}$	$\begin{array}{r}15\\-8\\\hline\end{array}$	$\begin{array}{r}9\\+8\\\hline\end{array}$	$\begin{array}{r}12\\-5\\\hline\end{array}$

G	$\begin{array}{r}15\\-6\\\hline\end{array}$	$\begin{array}{r}9\\-3\\\hline\end{array}$	$\begin{array}{r}18\\-9\\\hline\end{array}$	$\begin{array}{r}11\\-4\\\hline\end{array}$	$\begin{array}{r}10\\-9\\\hline\end{array}$	$\begin{array}{r}8\\-5\\\hline\end{array}$

Daily Facts Practice

A	9 −4	11 −3	17 −9	13 −7	8 −8	10 −6

B	8 +8	3 +7	9 +3	8 +6	4 +5	1 +9

C	12 −9	8 −2	11 −6	5 +4	9 +2	7 +7

D	10)‾80‾	8)‾72‾	6)‾18‾	4)‾20‾	12)‾48‾	9)‾54‾

E	5 +8	4 +7	8 +9	7 +5	2 +9	6 +8

F	13 −4	7 +3	8 −6	5 +5	13 −8	9 +4

G	6 −2	11 −8	15 −7	9 −5	20 −10	10 −2

Daily Facts Practice

A	11 ×12	4 ×9	5 ×6	11 ×8	4 ×4	3 ×6
B	6 ×12	8 ×9	5 ×4	3)‾27‾	12)‾132‾	9)‾45‾
C	3 +9	13 −9	6 −4	7 +10	14 −5	11 −7
D	16 −8	6 +5	7 +2	8 +7	10 −3	2 +8
E	7 +9	3 +1	8 +4	6 +3	2 +7	5 +7
F	7 −4	16 −7	9 −2	12 −8	7 −5	8 −3
G	7 +8	12 −3	3 +6	14 −9	9 +6	6 +4

Daily Facts Practice

A	2 +6	7 −2	7 +6	4 +8	11 −6	1 +7
B	9 −7	13 −10	12 −4	9 −6	14 −8	4 −2
C	5 +9	5 +6	8 +2	1 +6	3 +5	4 +4
D	5 −3	11 −8	12 −6	19 −10	9 −8	13 −4
E	13 −9	12 −7	7 −6	11 −6	10 −2	9 −1
F	10 +6	15 −10	3 +4	7 −5	8 +9	10 −3
G	9 −7	5 +2	11 −6	9 +7	12 −9	6 +6

Daily Facts Practice

A	$6 \atop \times 8$	$3 \atop \times 7$	$10 \atop \times 12$	$11 \atop \times 3$	$8 \atop \times 4$	$5 \atop \times 9$
B	$2 \atop \times 3$	$6 \atop \times 7$	$5 \atop \times 12$	$9 \atop \times 3$	$8 \atop \times 10$	$11 \atop \times 5$
C	$3 \atop \times 5$	$8 \atop \times 7$	$3 \atop \times 12$	$6 \atop \times 6$	$0 \atop \times 8$	$7 \atop \times 9$
D	$4 \atop \times 6$	$12 \overline{)108}$	$10 \atop \times 8$	$1 \overline{)6}$	$8 \atop \times 6$	$8 \overline{)24}$
E	$6 \overline{)18}$	$5 \atop \times 3$	$5 \overline{)15}$	$9 \atop \times 8$	$11 \overline{)33}$	$5 \atop \times 5$
F	$8 \overline{)64}$	$12 \overline{)72}$	$6 \overline{)42}$	$3 \overline{)9}$	$10 \overline{)90}$	$7 \overline{)35}$
G	$7 \overline{)21}$	$5 \overline{)30}$	$12 \overline{)144}$	$4 \overline{)32}$	$2 \overline{)24}$	$10 \overline{)10}$

Daily Facts Practice

A	$4\overline{)12}$	$12\overline{)120}$	$2\overline{)8}$	$6\overline{)54}$	$9\overline{)36}$	$5\overline{)40}$
B	$\begin{array}{r}4\\\times6\\\hline\end{array}$	$\begin{array}{r}5\\\times12\\\hline\end{array}$	$\begin{array}{r}7\\\times3\\\hline\end{array}$	$4\overline{)24}$	$8\overline{)40}$	$3\overline{)21}$
C	$\begin{array}{r}5\\+10\\\hline\end{array}$	$\begin{array}{r}2\\+4\\\hline\end{array}$	$\begin{array}{r}7\\+2\\\hline\end{array}$	$\begin{array}{r}5\\+8\\\hline\end{array}$	$\begin{array}{r}4\\+5\\\hline\end{array}$	$\begin{array}{r}9\\+3\\\hline\end{array}$
D	$\begin{array}{r}2\\+2\\\hline\end{array}$	$\begin{array}{r}8\\+8\\\hline\end{array}$	$\begin{array}{r}5\\+5\\\hline\end{array}$	$\begin{array}{r}7\\+7\\\hline\end{array}$	$\begin{array}{r}4\\+4\\\hline\end{array}$	$\begin{array}{r}9\\+9\\\hline\end{array}$
E	$\begin{array}{r}16\\-9\\\hline\end{array}$	$\begin{array}{r}13\\-5\\\hline\end{array}$	$\begin{array}{r}11\\-2\\\hline\end{array}$	$\begin{array}{r}4\\-4\\\hline\end{array}$	$\begin{array}{r}10\\-4\\\hline\end{array}$	$\begin{array}{r}14\\-7\\\hline\end{array}$
F	$\begin{array}{r}9\\-6\\\hline\end{array}$	$\begin{array}{r}8\\-4\\\hline\end{array}$	$\begin{array}{r}15\\-8\\\hline\end{array}$	$\begin{array}{r}7\\-3\\\hline\end{array}$	$\begin{array}{r}17\\-8\\\hline\end{array}$	$\begin{array}{r}11\\-10\\\hline\end{array}$
G	$\begin{array}{r}17\\-9\\\hline\end{array}$	$\begin{array}{r}4\\+9\\\hline\end{array}$	$\begin{array}{r}12\\-8\\\hline\end{array}$	$\begin{array}{r}2\\+7\\\hline\end{array}$	$\begin{array}{r}15\\-6\\\hline\end{array}$	$\begin{array}{r}6\\+7\\\hline\end{array}$

© Harcourt

Daily Facts Practice

A	2 +8	4 +3	15 −7	8 +6	11 −4	6 −2
B	2 +3	6 −3	5 −0	7 +4	8 +10	13 −6
C	10 ×9	6 ×6	7 ×5	8 ×12	7 ×11	12 ×9
D	3 ×9	5 ×10	12 ×12	6 ×7	8 ×0	12 ×2
E	9 ×12	7)56	5)25	1 ×7	12)60	3 ×3
F	12)132	11 ×11	10)0	0 ×10	8)48	6 ×8
G	10)70	4)8	2)12	6)54	11)44	9)81

Daily Facts Practice

A	$11\overline{)132}$	$9\overline{)54}$	$5\overline{)10}$	$7\overline{)63}$	$5\overline{)30}$	$3\overline{)0}$
B	$\begin{array}{r} 3 \\ +10 \\ \hline \end{array}$	$\begin{array}{r} 2 \\ +3 \\ \hline \end{array}$	$\begin{array}{r} 6 \\ +4 \\ \hline \end{array}$	$\begin{array}{r} 5 \\ +7 \\ \hline \end{array}$	$\begin{array}{r} 3 \\ +8 \\ \hline \end{array}$	$\begin{array}{r} 7 \\ +6 \\ \hline \end{array}$
C	$\begin{array}{r} 5 \\ -2 \\ \hline \end{array}$	$\begin{array}{r} 3 \\ +6 \\ \hline \end{array}$	$\begin{array}{r} 9 \\ -4 \\ \hline \end{array}$	$\begin{array}{r} 14 \\ -8 \\ \hline \end{array}$	$\begin{array}{r} 0 \\ +10 \\ \hline \end{array}$	$\begin{array}{r} 10 \\ -7 \\ \hline \end{array}$
D	$\begin{array}{r} 7 \\ -4 \\ \hline \end{array}$	$\begin{array}{r} 18 \\ -9 \\ \hline \end{array}$	$\begin{array}{r} 14 \\ -9 \\ \hline \end{array}$	$\begin{array}{r} 8 \\ -2 \\ \hline \end{array}$	$\begin{array}{r} 15 \\ -10 \\ \hline \end{array}$	$\begin{array}{r} 9 \\ -5 \\ \hline \end{array}$
E	$\begin{array}{r} 6 \\ -1 \\ \hline \end{array}$	$\begin{array}{r} 15 \\ -9 \\ \hline \end{array}$	$\begin{array}{r} 14 \\ -6 \\ \hline \end{array}$	$\begin{array}{r} 6 \\ -4 \\ \hline \end{array}$	$\begin{array}{r} 11 \\ -3 \\ \hline \end{array}$	$\begin{array}{r} 14 \\ -5 \\ \hline \end{array}$
F	$\begin{array}{r} 9 \\ +8 \\ \hline \end{array}$	$\begin{array}{r} 6 \\ +9 \\ \hline \end{array}$	$\begin{array}{r} 8 \\ +4 \\ \hline \end{array}$	$\begin{array}{r} 3 \\ +7 \\ \hline \end{array}$	$\begin{array}{r} 5 \\ +9 \\ \hline \end{array}$	$\begin{array}{r} 4 \\ +2 \\ \hline \end{array}$
G	$\begin{array}{r} 6 \\ +2 \\ \hline \end{array}$	$\begin{array}{r} 5 \\ +6 \\ \hline \end{array}$	$\begin{array}{r} 3 \\ +5 \\ \hline \end{array}$	$\begin{array}{r} 9 \\ +2 \\ \hline \end{array}$	$\begin{array}{r} 7 \\ +1 \\ \hline \end{array}$	$\begin{array}{r} 8 \\ +3 \\ \hline \end{array}$

Daily Facts Practice

A	6 +9	3 +3	7 +5	10 −6	8 −3	14 −7
B	2 +9	8 +5	6 +3	2 +5	4 +7	7 +8
C	6 +0	8 +2	7 +9	5 +4	9 +4	3 +4
D	11 −7	3 −2	12 −5	16 −7	13 −8	12 −3
E	16 −8	9 −2	8 −7	11 −9	12 −6	9 −3
F	4 +8	8 −6	6 +5	13 −7	5 +3	7 −2
G	3 +9	7 +3	10 +1	10 −8	12 −4	16 −9

Daily Facts Practice

A	$\begin{array}{r} 10 \\ \times 11 \\ \hline \end{array}$	$11\overline{)66}$	$4\overline{)40}$	$\begin{array}{r} 1 \\ \times 8 \\ \hline \end{array}$	$3\overline{)12}$	$7\overline{)14}$
B	$\begin{array}{r} 12 \\ \times 8 \\ \hline \end{array}$	$\begin{array}{r} 6 \\ \times 3 \\ \hline \end{array}$	$\begin{array}{r} 5 \\ \times 11 \\ \hline \end{array}$	$\begin{array}{r} 6 \\ \times 9 \\ \hline \end{array}$	$\begin{array}{r} 12 \\ \times 11 \\ \hline \end{array}$	$\begin{array}{r} 4 \\ \times 8 \\ \hline \end{array}$
C	$\begin{array}{r} 2 \\ \times 9 \\ \hline \end{array}$	$\begin{array}{r} 8 \\ \times 4 \\ \hline \end{array}$	$\begin{array}{r} 9 \\ \times 7 \\ \hline \end{array}$	$\begin{array}{r} 6 \\ \times 5 \\ \hline \end{array}$	$\begin{array}{r} 3 \\ \times 12 \\ \hline \end{array}$	$\begin{array}{r} 4 \\ \times 4 \\ \hline \end{array}$
D	$9\overline{)18}$	$4\overline{)16}$	$12\overline{)84}$	$8\overline{)8}$	$7\overline{)21}$	$11\overline{)110}$
E	$3\overline{)15}$	$6\overline{)66}$	$8\overline{)24}$	$6\overline{)48}$	$4\overline{)24}$	$3\overline{)6}$
F	$9\overline{)72}$	$7\overline{)42}$	$12\overline{)108}$	$\begin{array}{r} 8 \\ \times 6 \\ \hline \end{array}$	$\begin{array}{r} 5 \\ \times 4 \\ \hline \end{array}$	$\begin{array}{r} 7 \\ \times 8 \\ \hline \end{array}$
G	$11\overline{)121}$	$\begin{array}{r} 4 \\ \times 12 \\ \hline \end{array}$	$6\overline{)24}$	$\begin{array}{r} 9 \\ \times 3 \\ \hline \end{array}$	$3\overline{)27}$	$\begin{array}{r} 2 \\ \times 2 \\ \hline \end{array}$

Daily Facts Practice

A	8 −5	18 −9	7 −7	3 −0	17 −10	10 −5

B	2 +6	9 +5	10 +9	4 +6	8 +7	6 +8

C	2 +5	4 +3	6 +1	8 −4	11 −7	5 −1

D	7 ×12	4 ×7	8)72	4)28	8 ×8	3)18

E	9 ×12	3 ×8	12 ×3	6 ×10	9 ×5	6 ×4

F	6)32	9)63	8)64	5)40	12)72	7)28

G	11)22	8)40	5)60	4)20	8)96	7)49

Daily Facts Practice

A	$\begin{array}{r} 5 \\ \times 12 \\ \hline \end{array}$	$7\overline{)35}$	$\begin{array}{r} 8 \\ \times 3 \\ \hline \end{array}$	$9\overline{)81}$	$\begin{array}{r} 7 \\ \times 9 \\ \hline \end{array}$	$6\overline{)72}$
B	$\begin{array}{r} 12 \\ \times 6 \\ \hline \end{array}$	$\begin{array}{r} 4 \\ \times 5 \\ \hline \end{array}$	$\begin{array}{r} 2 \\ \times 7 \\ \hline \end{array}$	$\begin{array}{r} 3 \\ \times 11 \\ \hline \end{array}$	$\begin{array}{r} 5 \\ \times 8 \\ \hline \end{array}$	$\begin{array}{r} 3 \\ \times 9 \\ \hline \end{array}$
C	$\begin{array}{r} 8 \\ \times 9 \\ \hline \end{array}$	$\begin{array}{r} 12 \\ \times 7 \\ \hline \end{array}$	$\begin{array}{r} 6 \\ \times 8 \\ \hline \end{array}$	$\begin{array}{r} 7 \\ \times 4 \\ \hline \end{array}$	$\begin{array}{r} 11 \\ \times 11 \\ \hline \end{array}$	$\begin{array}{r} 8 \\ \times 7 \\ \hline \end{array}$
D	$9\overline{)36}$	$6\overline{)36}$	$8\overline{)56}$	$\begin{array}{r} 7 \\ \times 5 \\ \hline \end{array}$	$\begin{array}{r} 9 \\ \times 8 \\ \hline \end{array}$	$\begin{array}{r} 2 \\ \times 11 \\ \hline \end{array}$
E	$\begin{array}{r} 9 \\ +3 \\ \hline \end{array}$	$\begin{array}{r} 0 \\ +8 \\ \hline \end{array}$	$\begin{array}{r} 2 \\ +4 \\ \hline \end{array}$	$\begin{array}{r} 6 \\ +6 \\ \hline \end{array}$	$\begin{array}{r} 6 \\ +9 \\ \hline \end{array}$	$\begin{array}{r} 8 \\ +6 \\ \hline \end{array}$
F	$\begin{array}{r} 5 \\ -2 \\ \hline \end{array}$	$\begin{array}{r} 16 \\ -9 \\ \hline \end{array}$	$\begin{array}{r} 14 \\ -10 \\ \hline \end{array}$	$\begin{array}{r} 13 \\ -8 \\ \hline \end{array}$	$\begin{array}{r} 10 \\ -3 \\ \hline \end{array}$	$\begin{array}{r} 15 \\ -6 \\ \hline \end{array}$
G	$12\overline{)144}$	$9\overline{)27}$	$7\overline{)56}$	$5\overline{)35}$	$8\overline{)32}$	$11\overline{)110}$

Daily Facts Practice

A	$\begin{array}{r} 5 \\ \times 7 \\ \hline \end{array}$	$\begin{array}{r} 8 \\ \times 12 \\ \hline \end{array}$	$\begin{array}{r} 4 \\ \times 9 \\ \hline \end{array}$	$\begin{array}{r} 8 \\ \times 5 \\ \hline \end{array}$	$\begin{array}{r} 9 \\ \times 6 \\ \hline \end{array}$	$\begin{array}{r} 7 \\ \times 3 \\ \hline \end{array}$
B	$\begin{array}{r} 7 \\ \times 6 \\ \hline \end{array}$	$\begin{array}{r} 3 \\ \times 5 \\ \hline \end{array}$	$12\overline{)48}$	$6\overline{)42}$	$\begin{array}{r} 12 \\ \times 5 \\ \hline \end{array}$	$\begin{array}{r} 9 \\ \times 9 \\ \hline \end{array}$
C	$\begin{array}{r} 3 \\ +2 \\ \hline \end{array}$	$\begin{array}{r} 6 \\ +4 \\ \hline \end{array}$	$\begin{array}{r} 9 \\ +6 \\ \hline \end{array}$	$\begin{array}{r} 4 \\ +8 \\ \hline \end{array}$	$\begin{array}{r} 3 \\ +9 \\ \hline \end{array}$	$\begin{array}{r} 9 \\ +5 \\ \hline \end{array}$
D	$\begin{array}{r} 9 \\ +8 \\ \hline \end{array}$	$\begin{array}{r} 17 \\ -8 \\ \hline \end{array}$	$\begin{array}{r} 11 \\ -4 \\ \hline \end{array}$	$\begin{array}{r} 7 \\ +6 \\ \hline \end{array}$	$\begin{array}{r} 14 \\ -6 \\ \hline \end{array}$	$\begin{array}{r} 8 \\ -2 \\ \hline \end{array}$
E	$\begin{array}{r} 8 \\ +9 \\ \hline \end{array}$	$\begin{array}{r} 6 \\ +5 \\ \hline \end{array}$	$\begin{array}{r} 8 \\ +3 \\ \hline \end{array}$	$\begin{array}{r} 7 \\ +7 \\ \hline \end{array}$	$\begin{array}{r} 5 \\ +2 \\ \hline \end{array}$	$\begin{array}{r} 9 \\ +10 \\ \hline \end{array}$
F	$\begin{array}{r} 16 \\ -10 \\ \hline \end{array}$	$\begin{array}{r} 14 \\ -9 \\ \hline \end{array}$	$\begin{array}{r} 12 \\ -5 \\ \hline \end{array}$	$\begin{array}{r} 8 \\ -3 \\ \hline \end{array}$	$\begin{array}{r} 13 \\ -4 \\ \hline \end{array}$	$\begin{array}{r} 9 \\ -5 \\ \hline \end{array}$
G	$\begin{array}{r} 10 \\ -9 \\ \hline \end{array}$	$\begin{array}{r} 11 \\ -3 \\ \hline \end{array}$	$\begin{array}{r} 14 \\ -8 \\ \hline \end{array}$	$\begin{array}{r} 16 \\ -7 \\ \hline \end{array}$	$\begin{array}{r} 15 \\ -8 \\ \hline \end{array}$	$\begin{array}{r} 11 \\ -6 \\ \hline \end{array}$

Daily Facts Practice

A	9 $+7$	8 $+5$	5 $+7$	12 -9	13 -6	12 -4
B	5 $\times 6$	$5\overline{)45}$	$4\overline{)36}$	$11\overline{)132}$	7 $\times 7$	6 $\times 12$
C	3 $\times 6$	11 $\times 12$	9 $\times 10$	3 $\times 7$	5 $\times 9$	12 $\times 5$
D	$6\overline{)18}$	$3\overline{)21}$	$12\overline{)120}$	$8\overline{)80}$	$11\overline{)77}$	$3\overline{)24}$
E	12 $\times 12$	9 $\times 4$	11 $\times 5$	$12\overline{)96}$	$4\overline{)32}$	$11\overline{)0}$

$\begin{array}{r}0\\\times 0\\\hline\end{array}$	$\begin{array}{r}1\\\times 0\\\hline\end{array}$	$\begin{array}{r}2\\\times 0\\\hline\end{array}$
$\begin{array}{r}3\\\times 0\\\hline\end{array}$	$\begin{array}{r}4\\\times 0\\\hline\end{array}$	$\begin{array}{r}5\\\times 0\\\hline\end{array}$
$\begin{array}{r}6\\\times 0\\\hline\end{array}$	$\begin{array}{r}7\\\times 0\\\hline\end{array}$	$\begin{array}{r}8\\\times 0\\\hline\end{array}$

$$9 \times 0$$

$$10 \times 0$$

$$11 \times 0$$

$$12 \times 0$$

$$0 \times 1$$

$$1 \times 1$$

$$2 \times 1$$

$$3 \times 1$$

$$4 \times 1$$

5 ×1 ___	6 ×1 ___	7 ×1 ___
8 ×1 ___	9 ×1 ___	10 ×1 ___
11 ×1 ___	12 ×1 ___	0 ×2 ___

$$\begin{array}{r} 1 \\ \times 2 \\ \hline \end{array}$$

$$\begin{array}{r} 2 \\ \times 2 \\ \hline \end{array}$$

$$\begin{array}{r} 3 \\ \times 2 \\ \hline \end{array}$$

$$\begin{array}{r} 4 \\ \times 2 \\ \hline \end{array}$$

$$\begin{array}{r} 5 \\ \times 2 \\ \hline \end{array}$$

$$\begin{array}{r} 6 \\ \times 2 \\ \hline \end{array}$$

$$\begin{array}{r} 7 \\ \times 2 \\ \hline \end{array}$$

$$\begin{array}{r} 8 \\ \times 2 \\ \hline \end{array}$$

$$\begin{array}{r} 9 \\ \times 2 \\ \hline \end{array}$$

10	11	12
× 2	× 2	× 2

0	1	2
× 3	× 3	× 3

3	4	5
× 3	× 3	× 3

© Harcourt

Fact Cards

6 ×3	7 ×3	8 ×3
9 ×3	10 ×3	11 ×3
12 ×3	0 ×4	1 ×4

Fact Cards

$$\begin{array}{r} 2 \\ \times\ 4 \\ \hline \end{array}$$

$$\begin{array}{r} 3 \\ \times\ 4 \\ \hline \end{array}$$

$$\begin{array}{r} 4 \\ \times\ 4 \\ \hline \end{array}$$

$$\begin{array}{r} 5 \\ \times\ 4 \\ \hline \end{array}$$

$$\begin{array}{r} 6 \\ \times\ 4 \\ \hline \end{array}$$

$$\begin{array}{r} 7 \\ \times\ 4 \\ \hline \end{array}$$

$$\begin{array}{r} 8 \\ \times\ 4 \\ \hline \end{array}$$

$$\begin{array}{r} 9 \\ \times\ 4 \\ \hline \end{array}$$

$$\begin{array}{r} 10 \\ \times\ 4 \\ \hline \end{array}$$

$$\begin{array}{r} 11 \\ \times 4 \\ \hline \end{array}$$

$$\begin{array}{r} 12 \\ \times 4 \\ \hline \end{array}$$

$$\begin{array}{r} 0 \\ \times 5 \\ \hline \end{array}$$

$$\begin{array}{r} 1 \\ \times 5 \\ \hline \end{array}$$

$$\begin{array}{r} 2 \\ \times 5 \\ \hline \end{array}$$

$$\begin{array}{r} 3 \\ \times 5 \\ \hline \end{array}$$

$$\begin{array}{r} 4 \\ \times 5 \\ \hline \end{array}$$

$$\begin{array}{r} 5 \\ \times 5 \\ \hline \end{array}$$

$$\begin{array}{r} 6 \\ \times 5 \\ \hline \end{array}$$

$$\begin{array}{r}7\\ \times 5\\ \hline\end{array}$$

$$\begin{array}{r}8\\ \times 5\\ \hline\end{array}$$

$$\begin{array}{r}9\\ \times 5\\ \hline\end{array}$$

$$\begin{array}{r}10\\ \times 5\\ \hline\end{array}$$

$$\begin{array}{r}11\\ \times 5\\ \hline\end{array}$$

$$\begin{array}{r}12\\ \times 5\\ \hline\end{array}$$

$$\begin{array}{r}0\\ \times 6\\ \hline\end{array}$$

$$\begin{array}{r}1\\ \times 6\\ \hline\end{array}$$

$$\begin{array}{r}2\\ \times 6\\ \hline\end{array}$$

$$\begin{array}{r} 3 \\ \times 6 \\ \hline \end{array}$$

$$\begin{array}{r} 4 \\ \times 6 \\ \hline \end{array}$$

$$\begin{array}{r} 5 \\ \times 6 \\ \hline \end{array}$$

$$\begin{array}{r} 6 \\ \times 6 \\ \hline \end{array}$$

$$\begin{array}{r} 7 \\ \times 6 \\ \hline \end{array}$$

$$\begin{array}{r} 8 \\ \times 6 \\ \hline \end{array}$$

$$\begin{array}{r} 9 \\ \times 6 \\ \hline \end{array}$$

$$\begin{array}{r} 10 \\ \times 6 \\ \hline \end{array}$$

$$\begin{array}{r} 11 \\ \times 6 \\ \hline \end{array}$$

12	0	1
×6	×7	×7
————	————	————

2	3	4
×7	×7	×7
————	————	————

5	6	7
×7	×7	×7
————	————	————

8 × 7	9 × 7	10 × 7
11 × 7	12 × 7	0 × 8
1 × 8	2 × 8	3 × 8

$$\begin{array}{r} 4 \\ \times\ 8 \\ \hline \end{array}$$

$$\begin{array}{r} 5 \\ \times\ 8 \\ \hline \end{array}$$

$$\begin{array}{r} 6 \\ \times\ 8 \\ \hline \end{array}$$

$$\begin{array}{r} 7 \\ \times\ 8 \\ \hline \end{array}$$

$$\begin{array}{r} 8 \\ \times\ 8 \\ \hline \end{array}$$

$$\begin{array}{r} 9 \\ \times\ 8 \\ \hline \end{array}$$

$$\begin{array}{r} 10 \\ \times\ 8 \\ \hline \end{array}$$

$$\begin{array}{r} 11 \\ \times\ 8 \\ \hline \end{array}$$

$$\begin{array}{r} 12 \\ \times\ 8 \\ \hline \end{array}$$

Fact Cards

$$\begin{array}{r} 0 \\ \times\,9 \\ \hline \end{array}$$

$$\begin{array}{r} 1 \\ \times\,9 \\ \hline \end{array}$$

$$\begin{array}{r} 2 \\ \times\,9 \\ \hline \end{array}$$

$$\begin{array}{r} 3 \\ \times\,9 \\ \hline \end{array}$$

$$\begin{array}{r} 4 \\ \times\,9 \\ \hline \end{array}$$

$$\begin{array}{r} 5 \\ \times\,9 \\ \hline \end{array}$$

$$\begin{array}{r} 6 \\ \times\,9 \\ \hline \end{array}$$

$$\begin{array}{r} 7 \\ \times\,9 \\ \hline \end{array}$$

$$\begin{array}{r} 8 \\ \times\,9 \\ \hline \end{array}$$

$$\begin{array}{r} 9 \\ \times\, 9 \\ \hline \end{array}$$

$$\begin{array}{r} 10 \\ \times\, 9 \\ \hline \end{array}$$

$$\begin{array}{r} 11 \\ \times\, 9 \\ \hline \end{array}$$

$$\begin{array}{r} 12 \\ \times\, 9 \\ \hline \end{array}$$

$$\begin{array}{r} 0 \\ \times\, 10 \\ \hline \end{array}$$

$$\begin{array}{r} 1 \\ \times\, 10 \\ \hline \end{array}$$

$$\begin{array}{r} 2 \\ \times\, 10 \\ \hline \end{array}$$

$$\begin{array}{r} 3 \\ \times\, 10 \\ \hline \end{array}$$

$$\begin{array}{r} 4 \\ \times\, 10 \\ \hline \end{array}$$

$$\begin{array}{r} 5 \\ \times\,10 \\ \hline \end{array}$$

$$\begin{array}{r} 6 \\ \times\,10 \\ \hline \end{array}$$

$$\begin{array}{r} 7 \\ \times\,10 \\ \hline \end{array}$$

$$\begin{array}{r} 8 \\ \times\,10 \\ \hline \end{array}$$

$$\begin{array}{r} 9 \\ \times\,10 \\ \hline \end{array}$$

$$\begin{array}{r} 10 \\ \times\,10 \\ \hline \end{array}$$

$$\begin{array}{r} 11 \\ \times\,10 \\ \hline \end{array}$$

$$\begin{array}{r} 12 \\ \times\,10 \\ \hline \end{array}$$

$$\begin{array}{r} 0 \\ \times\,11 \\ \hline \end{array}$$

$$\begin{array}{r} 1 \\ \times 11 \\ \hline \end{array}$$

$$\begin{array}{r} 2 \\ \times 11 \\ \hline \end{array}$$

$$\begin{array}{r} 3 \\ \times 11 \\ \hline \end{array}$$

$$\begin{array}{r} 4 \\ \times 11 \\ \hline \end{array}$$

$$\begin{array}{r} 5 \\ \times 11 \\ \hline \end{array}$$

$$\begin{array}{r} 6 \\ \times 11 \\ \hline \end{array}$$

$$\begin{array}{r} 7 \\ \times 11 \\ \hline \end{array}$$

$$\begin{array}{r} 8 \\ \times 11 \\ \hline \end{array}$$

$$\begin{array}{r} 9 \\ \times 11 \\ \hline \end{array}$$

10 × 11	11 × 11	12 × 11
0 × 12	1 × 12	2 × 12
3 × 12	4 × 12	5 × 12

© Harcourt

$$\begin{array}{r} 6 \\ \times\ 12 \\ \hline \end{array}$$

$$\begin{array}{r} 7 \\ \times\ 12 \\ \hline \end{array}$$

$$\begin{array}{r} 8 \\ \times\ 12 \\ \hline \end{array}$$

$$\begin{array}{r} 9 \\ \times\ 12 \\ \hline \end{array}$$

$$\begin{array}{r} 10 \\ \times\ 12 \\ \hline \end{array}$$

$$\begin{array}{r} 11 \\ \times\ 12 \\ \hline \end{array}$$

$$\begin{array}{r} 12 \\ \times\ 12 \\ \hline \end{array}$$

Fact Cards

$1 \overline{)2}$

$1 \overline{)5}$

$1 \overline{)8}$

$1 \overline{)1}$

$1 \overline{)4}$

$1 \overline{)7}$

$1 \overline{)0}$

$1 \overline{)3}$

$1 \overline{)6}$

$1\overline{)11}$

$2\overline{)2}$

$2\overline{)8}$

$1\overline{)10}$

$2\overline{)0}$

$2\overline{)6}$

$1\overline{)9}$

$1\overline{)12}$

$2\overline{)4}$

2)14

2)20

3)0

2)12

2)18

2)24

2)10

2)16

2)22

$3\overline{)9}$

$3\overline{)18}$

$3\overline{)27}$

$3\overline{)6}$

$3\overline{)15}$

$3\overline{)24}$

$3\overline{)3}$

$3\overline{)12}$

$3\overline{)21}$

$3\overline{)36}$

$4\overline{)8}$

$4\overline{)20}$

$3\overline{)33}$

$4\overline{)4}$

$4\overline{)16}$

$3\overline{)30}$

$4\overline{)0}$

$4\overline{)12}$

$4\overline{)32}$

$4\overline{)44}$

$5\overline{)5}$

$4\overline{)28}$

$4\overline{)40}$

$5\overline{)0}$

$4\overline{)24}$

$4\overline{)36}$

$4\overline{)48}$

Fact Cards

$5\overline{)20}$	$5\overline{)35}$	$5\overline{)50}$
$5\overline{)15}$	$5\overline{)30}$	$5\overline{)45}$
$5\overline{)10}$	$5\overline{)25}$	$5\overline{)40}$

6)0

6)18

6)36

5)60

6)12

6)30

5)55

6)6

6)24

Fact Cards

6)54

6)72

7)14

6)48

6)66

7)7

6)42

6)60

7)0

Fact Cards

7)35

7)56

7)77

7)28

7)49

7)70

7)21

7)42

7)63

© Harcourt

$8 \overline{)8}$

$8 \overline{)32}$

$8 \overline{)56}$

$8 \overline{)0}$

$8 \overline{)24}$

$8 \overline{)48}$

$7 \overline{)84}$

$8 \overline{)16}$

$8 \overline{)40}$

$8\overline{)80}$

$9\overline{)0}$

$9\overline{)27}$

$8\overline{)72}$

$8\overline{)96}$

$9\overline{)18}$

$8\overline{)64}$

$8\overline{)88}$

$9\overline{)9}$

$9\overline{)54}$

$9\overline{)81}$

$9\overline{)108}$

$9\overline{)45}$

$9\overline{)72}$

$9\overline{)99}$

$9\overline{)36}$

$9\overline{)63}$

$9\overline{)90}$

$10\overline{)20}$

$10\overline{)50}$

$10\overline{)80}$

$10\overline{)10}$

$10\overline{)40}$

$10\overline{)70}$

$10\overline{)0}$

$10\overline{)30}$

$10\overline{)60}$

Fact Cards

$10\overline{)110}$

$11\overline{)11}$

$11\overline{)44}$

$10\overline{)100}$

$11\overline{)0}$

$11\overline{)33}$

$10\overline{)90}$

$10\overline{)120}$

$11\overline{)22}$

$11\overline{)77}$

$11\overline{)110}$

$12\overline{)0}$

$11\overline{)66}$

$11\overline{)99}$

$11\overline{)132}$

$11\overline{)55}$

$11\overline{)88}$

$11\overline{)121}$

$12\overline{)36}$

$12\overline{)72}$

$12\overline{)108}$

$12\overline{)24}$

$12\overline{)60}$

$12\overline{)96}$

$12\overline{)12}$

$12\overline{)48}$

$12\overline{)84}$

$$12 \overline{)144}$$

$$12 \overline{)132}$$

$$12 \overline{)120}$$

Fact Cards

VOCABULARY CARDS

Use the vocabulary cards to practice and review this year's new math terms. Suggestions for using the cards are in the *Teacher's Edition,* on the Vocabulary Power page.

Consider having students organize their vocabulary cards in Math Word Files—containers made from zip-top bags or small boxes, such as crayon or computer disk boxes. Encourage students to consult their Math Word Files to confirm meanings, verify pronunciations, and check spellings.

To copy, set your machine to 2-sided copies. Align the perforated edge with the left-hand (or top) guide on the glass, and copy. Flip the page, align the perforated edge with the opposite (right-hand or bottom) guide, and copy.

Pronunciation Key

a	add, map	h	hope, hate	ô	order, jaw	ŧħ	this, bathe
ā	ace, rate	i	it, give	oi	oil, boy	u	up, done
â(r)	care, air	ī	ice, write	ou	pout, now	û(r)	burn, term
ä	palm, father	j	joy, ledge	o͝o	took, full	yo͞o	fuse, few
b	bat, rub	k	cool, take	o͞o	pool, food	v	vain, eve
ch	check, catch	l	look, rule	p	pit, stop	w	win, away
d	dog, rod	m	move, seem	r	run, poor	y	yet, yearn
e	end, pet	n	nice, tin	s	see, pass	z	zest, muse
ē	equal, tree	ng	ring, song	sh	sure, rush	zh	vision,
f	fit, half	o	odd, hot	t	talk, sit		pleasure
g	go, log	ō	open, so	th	thin, both		

ə   the schwa, an unstressed vowel representing the sound spelled *a* in **a**bove, *e* in sick**e**n, *i* in poss**i**ble, *o* in mel**o**n, *u* in circ**u**s

Other symbols:
* • separates words into syllables
* ′ indicates stress on a syllable

billion	**hundredth**
benchmark	**thousandth**
decimal	**ten-thousandth**
tenth	**equivalent decimals**

Vocabulary Cards

hun′drədth
One of one hundred equal parts

Chapter 2, Lesson 1

bil′yən
One thousand million; written 1,000,000,000

Chapter 1, Lesson 2

thou′zendth
One of one thousand equal parts

Chapter 2, Lesson 1

bench′märk
A familiar number used as a point of reference

Chapter 1, Lesson 3

ten thou′zendth
One of ten thousand equal parts

Chapter 2, Lesson 1

de′sə•məl
A number with one or more digits to the right of the decimal point

Chapter 2, Lesson 1

ē•kwiv′ə•lənt de′sə•məlz
Decimals that name the same number or amount

Chapter 2, Lesson 2

tenth
One of ten equal parts

Chapter 2, Lesson 1

estimate	equation
front-end estimation	solution
expression	inequality
variable	Commutative Property of Addition

i•kwā′zhən
An algebraic or numerical sentence that shows that two quantities are equal

Chapter 4, Lesson 2

es′tə•māt (verb)
To find a number that is close to an exact amount
es′tə•mət (noun)
A number close to an exact amount

Chapter 3, Lesson 3

sə•loo′shən
A value that, when substituted for the variable, makes an equation true

Chapter 4, Lesson 3

frunt end es•tə•mā′shən
A method of estimating sums or differences by using the value of the front digits of the numbers

Chapter 3, Lesson 3

in•i•kwä′lə•tē
A mathematical sentence that shows that two amounts are not equal

Chapter 4, Lesson 4

ik•spre′shən
A mathematical phrase or the part of a number sentence that combines numbers, operation signs, and sometimes variables, but doesn't have an equal sign

Chapter 4, Lesson 1

kə•myoo′tə•tiv prä′pər•tē əv ə•di′shən
The property that states that when the order of two addends is changed, the sum is the same

Chapter 4, Lesson 5

vâr′ē•ə•bəl
A letter or symbol that stands for one or more numbers

Chapter 4, Lesson 1

Vocabulary Cards

Associative Property of Addition	**population**
compensation	**random sample**
survey	**cumulative frequency**
sample	**outlier**

pä•pyə•lā′shən

The entire group of objects or individuals considered for a survey

ə•sō′shē•ə•tiv prä′pər•tē əv ə•di′shən

The property that states that when the grouping of addends is changed, the sum is the same

ran′dəm sam′pəl

A sample in which each subject in the overall population has an equal chance of being chosen

kom′pən•sā′shən

An estimation strategy in which you change one addend to a multiple of ten and then adjust the other addend to keep the balance

kyoo′myə•lə•tiv frē′kwən•sē

A running total of data

sûr′vā

A method of gathering information about a group

out′lī•ər

A value separated from the rest of the data

sam′pəl

A part of a population

mean	scale
median	interval
mode	ordered pair
stem-and-leaf plot	histogram

skāl

A series of numbers starting at zero and placed at fixed distances on a graph to help label the graph

Chapter 6, Lesson 1

mēn

The average of a set of numbers, found by dividing the sum of the set by the number of addends

Chapter 5, Lesson 2

in'tər•vəl

The distance between one number and the next on the scale of a graph

Chapter 6, Lesson 1

mē'dē•ən

The middle number in a set of data that are arranged in order

Chapter 5, Lesson 3

ôr'dərd pâr

A pair of numbers used to locate a point on a grid; the first number tells the left-right position, and the second number tells the up-down position

Chapter 6, Lesson 2

mōd

The number or item that occurs most often in a set of data

Chapter 5, Lesson 3

his'tə•gram

A bar graph that shows the number of times data occur within intervals

Chapter 6, Lesson 5

stem ənd lēf plot

A table that shows groups of data arranged by place value

Chapter 5, Lesson 4

multiple	function
compatible numbers	Commutative Property of Multiplication
evaluate	Associative Property of Multiplication
order of operations	Distributive Property

funk′shən
A relationship between two quantities in which one quantity depends on the other

Chapter 12, Lesson 4

mul′tə•pəl
The product of a given whole number and another whole number

Chapter 7, Lesson 1

kə•myoo′tə•tiv prä′pər•tē əv mul•tə•plə•kā′shən
The property that states that when the order of two factors is changed, the product is the same

Chapter 12, Lesson 6

kəm•pa′tə•bəl num′bərz
Numbers that are easy to compute mentally

Chapter 9, Lesson 1

ə•sō′shē•ə•tiv prä′pər•tē əv mul•tə•plə•kā′shən
The property that states that the way factors are grouped does not change the product

Chapter 12, Lesson 6

i•val′yə•wāt
To find the value of a numerical or algebraic expression

Chapter 12, Lesson 1

di•strib′yə•tiv prä′pər•tē
The property that states that multiplying a sum by a number is the same as multiplying each addend in the sum by the number and then adding the products

Chapter 12, Lesson 7

ôr′dər əv ä•pə•rā′shənz
Rules for performing operations in expressions with more than one operation; do the operations inside parentheses, then multiply and divide from left to right, then add and subtract from left to right

Chapter 12, Lesson 2

© Harcourt

divisible	exponent
greatest common factor (GCF)	base
common multiple	square number
least common multiple (LCM)	composite number

ek'spō•nənt
A number that shows how many times the base is used as a factor

Chapter 14, Lesson 1

də•vi'zi•bəl
Capable of being divided without a remainder

Chapter 13, Lesson 1

bās
A number used as a repeated factor

Chapter 14, Lesson 1

grā'təst kä'mən fak'tər
The greatest factor that two or more numbers have in common

Chapter 13, Lesson 2

skwâr num'bər
A product of a number and itself

Chapter 14, Lesson 1

kä'mən mul'tə•pəl
A number that is a multiple of two or more numbers

Chapter 13, Lesson 3

käm•pä'zət num'bər
A whole number having more than two factors, such as 6, whose factors are 1, 2, 3, and 6

Chapter 14, Lesson 3

lēst kä'mən mul'tə•pəl
The least number, other than zero, that is a common multiple of two or more numbers

Chapter 13, Lesson 3

prime number	simplest form
prime factorization	mixed number
factor tree	least common denominator (LCD)
equivalent fractions	reciprocal

© Harcourt

sim′pləst fôrm
The form of a fraction in which the numerator and denominator have only 1 as a common factor

Chapter 15, Lesson 2

prīm num′bər
A whole number that has exactly two factors: 1 and itself

Chapter 14, Lesson 3

mikst num′bər
A number that is made up of a whole number and a fraction

Chapter 15, Lesson 3

prīm fak•tə•ri•zā′shən
The process of factoring a composite number into its prime components, as with a factor tree, so that it is written as the product of all its prime factors

Chapter 14, Lesson 4

lēst kä′mən di•nä′mə•nā•tər
The least common multiple of two or more denominators

Chapter 16, Lesson 4

fak′tər trē
A diagram that shows the prime factors of a number

Chapter 14, Lesson 4

ri•sip′rə•kəl
One of two numbers whose product is 1;
$8 \times \frac{1}{8} = 1$

Chapter 19, Lesson 2

ē•kwiv′ə•lənt frak′shənz
Fractions that name the same number or amount

Chapter 15, Lesson 1

point	**plane**
line	**angle**
ray	**parallel lines**
line segment	**intersecting lines**

plān **A flat surface that extends without end in all directions** Chapter 20, Lesson 1	point **An exact location in space, usually represented by a dot** Chapter 20, Lesson 1
ang′gəl **A figure formed by two rays that meet at a common endpoint** Chapter 20, Lesson 1	līn **A straight path in a plane, extending in both directions with no endpoints** Chapter 20, Lesson 1
par′ə•lel līnz **Lines in a plane that do not intersect** Chapter 20, Lesson 1	rā **A part of a line; it begins at one endpoint and extends forever in one direction** Chapter 20, Lesson 1
in•tər•sek′ting līnz **Lines that cross each other at exactly one point** Chapter 20, Lesson 1	līn seg′mənt **A part of a line between two endpoints** Chapter 20, Lesson 1

perpendicular lines	regular polygon
degree	circle
protractor	radius
polygon	diameter

re′gyə•lər pä′lē•gän
A polygon in which all sides are congruent and all angles are congruent

Chapter 20, Lesson 3

pər•pən•dik′yə•lər līnz
Two lines that intersect to form right angles

Chapter 20, Lesson 1

sûr′kəl
A closed figure with all points on the figure the same distance from the center point

Chapter 20, Lesson 4

di•grē′
A unit for measuring angles or temperature

Chapter 20, Lesson 1

rā′dē•əs
A line segment with one endpoint at the center of a circle and the other endpoint on the circle

Chapter 20, Lesson 4

prō′trak•tər
A tool used for measuring or drawing angles

Chapter 20, Lesson 2

dī•am′ə•tər
A line segment that passes through the center of a circle and has its endpoints on the circle

Chapter 20, Lesson 4

pä′lē•gän
A closed plane figure formed by three or more line segments

Chapter 20, Lesson 3

chord	**similar**
compass	**corresponding angles**
central angle	**corresponding sides**
congruent	**line symmetry**

© Harcourt

si′mə•lər
Having the same shape but not necessarily the same size

Chapter 20, Lesson 5

kôrd
A line segment with endpoints on a circle

Chapter 20, Lesson 4

kôr•ə•spän′ding ang′gəlz
Angles that are in the same position in different figures

Chapter 20, Lesson 5

kum′pəs
A tool used to construct circles and arcs

Chapter 20, Lesson 4

kôr•ə•spän′ding sīdz
Sides that are in the same position in different plane figures

Chapter 20, Lesson 5

sen′trəl ang′gəl
An angle formed by two radii of a circle that meet at its center

Chapter 20, Lesson 4

līn si′mə•trē
The property of a figure that can be separated by a line into two congruent parts

Chapter 20, Lesson 6

kən•grŌŌ′ənt
Having the same size and shape

Chapter 20, Lesson 5

rotational symmetry	leg
isosceles triangle	hypotenuse
scalene triangle	figurate numbers
equilateral triangle	triangular numbers

leg

In a right triangle, either of the two sides that form the right angle

Chapter 21, Lesson 1

rō•tā′shən•əl si′mə•trē

The property of a figure that, when rotated less than 360° about a central point or a point of rotation, still matches the original figure

Chapter 20, Lesson 6

hī•pot′ə•nōōs

In a right triangle, the side opposite the right angle; the longest side in a right triangle

Chapter 21, Lesson 1

ī•sä′sə•lēz tri′ang•gəl

A triangle with exactly two congruent sides

Chapter 21, Lesson 1

fi′gyə•rət num′bərz

Numbers that can be represented by geometric figures

Chapter 21, Lesson 1

skā′lēn tri′ang•gəl

A triangle with no congruent sides

Chapter 21, Lesson 1

tri•ang′gyə•lər num′bərz

Numbers that can be represented by triangular figures

Chapter 21, Lesson 1

ē•kwə•la′tə•rəl tri′ang•gəl

A triangle with three congruent sides

Chapter 21, Lesson 1

Vocabulary Cards

trapezoid	reflection
rhombus	rotation
parallelogram	transformation
translation	tessellation

ri•flek′shən
A movement of a figure to a new position by flipping it over a line; a flip

Chapter 21, Lesson 3

tra′pə•zoid
A quadrilateral with exactly one pair of parallel sides

Chapter 21, Lesson 2

rō•tā′shən
A movement of a figure to a new position by turning it around a fixed point; a turn

Chapter 21, Lesson 3

räm′bəs
A parallelogram with congruent sides

Chapter 21, Lesson 2

trans•fər•mā′shən
The movement of a figure to a new position by a translation, reflection, or rotation

Chapter 21, Lesson 3

par•ə•lel′ə•gram
A quadrilateral whose opposite sides are parallel and congruent

Chapter 21, Lesson 2

tes•ə•lā′shən
A repeating pattern of closed figures that covers a surface with no gaps and no overlaps

Chapter 21, Lesson 3

trans•lā′shən
A movement of a figure to a new position along a straight line; a slide

Chapter 21, Lesson 3

polyhedron	integers
pyramid	negative integer
prism	positive integer
base	opposites

in′ti•jərz
The set of whole numbers and their opposites

Chapter 22, Lesson 1

pä•lē•hē′drən
A solid figure with faces that are polygons

Chapter 21, Lesson 4

ne′gə•tiv in′ti•jər
Any integer less than zero

Chapter 22, Lesson 1

pir′ə•mid
A solid figure with a polygon base and all other faces are triangles that meet at a common vertex

Chapter 21, Lesson 4

pä′zə•tiv in′ti•jər
Any integer greater than zero

Chapter 22, Lesson 1

priz′əm
A solid figure that has two congruent, polygon-shaped bases and whose other faces are all rectangles

Chapter 21, Lesson 4

ä′pə•zəts
Two numbers that are the same distance, but in opposite directions, from zero on a number line

Chapter 22, Lesson 1

bās
A polygon's side or a solid figure's face by which the figure is measured or named

Chapter 21, Lesson 4

absolute value	origin
x-axis	coordinates
y-axis	precision
coordinate plane	millimeter (mm)

© Harcourt

ôr′ə•jən
The point where the two axes of a coordinate plane intersect, (0,0)

Chapter 23, Lesson 2

ab•sə•lo͞ot′ val′yo͞o
The distance of a number from zero on a number line

Chapter 22, Lesson 1

kō•ôr′də•nəts
The numbers in an ordered pair

Chapter 23, Lesson 2

eks ak′səs
The horizontal number line on a coordinate plane

Chapter 23, Lesson 1

pri•sizh′ən
A property of measurement that is related to the unit of measure used; the smaller the unit of measure used, the more precise the measurement

Chapter 24, Lesson 1

wī ak′səs
The vertical number line on a coordinate plane

Chapter 23, Lesson 1

mi′lə•mē•tər
A metric unit for measuring length or distance; 1 millimeter = 0.001 meter

Chapter 24, Lesson 2

kō•ôr′də•nət plān
A plane formed by two intersecting and perpendicular number lines called axes

Chapter 23, Lesson 2

centimeter (cm)	Celsius (°C)
meter (m)	perimeter
kilometer (km)	circumference
Fahrenheit (°F)	area

sə l′sē•us
A metric unit for measuring temperature

Chapter 24, Lesson 6

sen′tə•mē•tər
A metric unit for measuring length or distance; 1 centimeter = 0.01 meter

Chapter 24, Lesson 2

pə•rim′ə•tər
The distance around a closed plane figure

Chapter 25, Lesson 1

mē′tər
A metric unit for measuring length or distance; 1 meter = 100 centimeters

Chapter 24, Lesson 2

sər•kum′fər•əns
The distance around a circle

Chapter 25, Lesson 4

kə•lä′mə•tər
A metric unit for measuring length or distance; 1 kilometer = 1000 meters

Chapter 24, Lesson 2

âr′ē•ə
The number of square units needed to cover a surface

Chapter 26, Lesson 1

fâr′ən•hīt
A customary unit for measuring temperature

Chapter 24, Lesson 6

base	volume
height	ratio
net	equivalent ratios
surface area	proportion

väl′yəm
The measure of the space a solid figure occupies

Chapter 27, Lesson 3

bās
A polygon's side or a solid figure's face by which the figure is measured or named

Chapter 26, Lesson 4

rā′shē•ō
The comparison of two quantities

Chapter 28, Lesson 2

hīt
The length of a perpendicular from the base to the top of a plane figure or a solid figure

Chapter 26, Lesson 4

ē•kwiv′ə•lənt rā′shē•ōz
Ratios that make the same comparison

Chapter 28, Lesson 3

net
A two-dimensional pattern that can be folded into a three-dimensional prism or pyramid

Chapter 27, Lesson 1

prə•pôr′shən
An equation that shows that two ratios are equal

Chapter 28, Lesson 3

sûr′fəs âr′ē•ə
The sum of the areas of all the faces, or surfaces, of a solid figure

Chapter 27, Lesson 2

Vocabulary Cards

scale drawing	sample space
map scale	possible outcomes
percent	theoretical probability
probability	equally likely

sam′pəl spās
The set of all possible outcomes

Chapter 30, Lesson 2

skāl drô′ing
A reduced or enlarged drawing whose shape is the same as an actual object and whose size is determined by the scale

Chapter 28, Lesson 4

pä′sə•bəl out′kumz
The events that have a chance of happening in an experiment

Chapter 30, Lesson 2

map skāl
A ratio that compares distance on a map with actual distance

Chapter 28, Lesson 4

thē•ə•re′ti•kəl prä•bə•bil′ə•tē
A comparison of the number of favorable outcomes to the number of possible equally likely outcomes

Chapter 30, Lesson 2

pər•sent′
A ratio of a number to 100

Chapter 29, Lesson 1

ē′kwəl•lē lī′klē
Having the same chance of occurring

Chapter 30, Lesson 2

prä•bə•bil′ə•tē
The likelihood that an event will happen

Chapter 30, Lesson 1

experimental probability	**pictograph**
tree diagram	**bar graph**
arrangement	**line graph**
combination	**circle graph**

pik′tə•graf
A graph that displays countable data with symbols or pictures

Chapter 5, Lesson 5

ik•sper•ə•men′•təl prä•bə•bil′ə•tē
The ratio of the number of times the event occurs to the total number of trials or times the activity is performed

Chapter 30, Lesson 3

bär graf
A graph that uses horizontal or vertical bars to display countable data

Chapter 5, Lesson 5

trē dī′ə•gram
An organized list that shows all possible outcomes for an event

Chapter 30, Lesson 4

līn graf
A graph that uses a line to show how data change over time

Chapter 5, Lesson 5

ə•rānj′mənt
An ordering of items

Chapter 30, Lesson 5

sər′kəl graf
A graph that shows how parts of the data are related to the whole and to each other

Chapter 5, Lesson 5

käm•bə•nā′shən
A choice in which the order of the items does not matter

Chapter 30, Lesson 5

IT'S IN THE BAG

This section's blackline masters accompany "It's in the Bag."
Directions for these and other fun "It's in the Bag" projects appear
in every unit of your *Harcourt Math* pupil's and teacher's editions.

Scavenger Hunt Tote

A ☐ Find a number that has the digit 4 in the ten thousands place.

B ☐ Find a fraction that is less than one half.

C ☐ Find a decimal that has a digit in the thousandths place.

D ☐ Find a mixed number that is greater than two and six tenths.

E ☐ Find a decimal that is equivalent to 1.5.

F ☐ Find a number that is rounded.

G ☐ Find a decimal that is between 5.75 and 8.75.

H ☐ Find an item that costs $450,000 more than $550,000.

I ☐ Find a phone number that has no repeating digits.

Shoot for the Moon

Playing the Game:

- The game is played in pairs. Each player takes turns rolling the number cube and moving the game piece.

- If the crater has instructions, use the spinner to represent the value of *n* in the expression. Then find the value of the expression. If the value is correct, move the correct number of spaces.

- If there are no instructions on the crater, it's the next player's turn.

- Players take turns until crater 20 is reached.

Shoot for the Moon

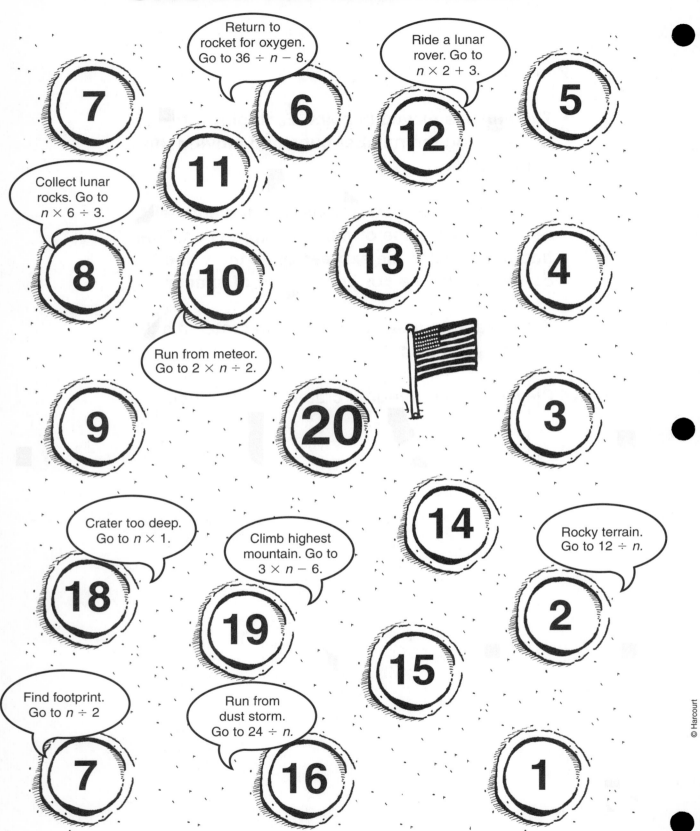

© Harcourt

Venn Diagrams

Title: _____

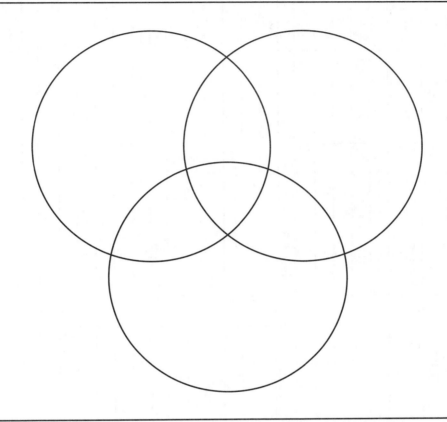

line up with bottom edge of protector

Cookbook Comparisons

Ingredients	Serves 12	Serves 16	Serves 24
Recipe 1			
Recipe 2			
Recipe 3			
Recipe 4			

Ingredients	Serves 12	Serves 16	Serves 24
Recipe 5			
Recipe 6			
Recipe 7			
Recipe 8			

Tessellation Puzzle

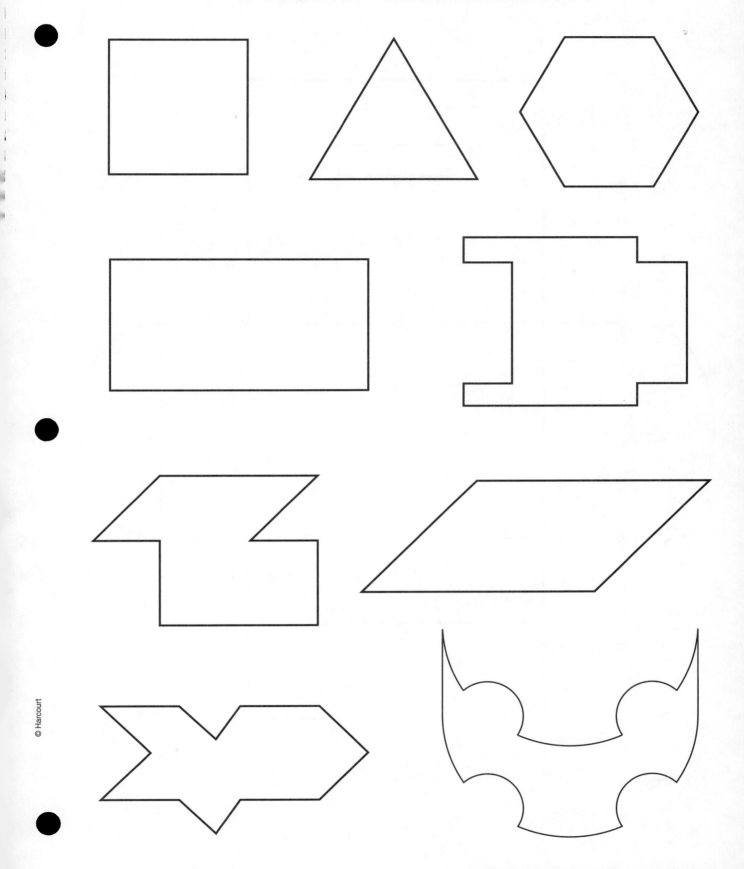

IT'S IN THE BAG • Unit 7   **Teacher's Resource Book   TR187**

From Net to Solid

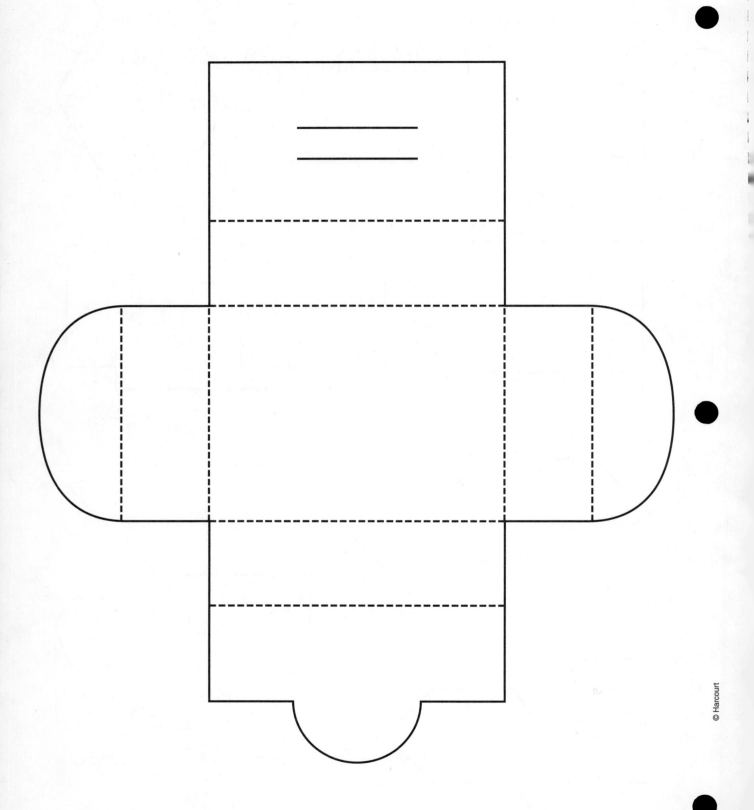

© Harcourt